# window
# treatments

# window treatments

A source book of contemporary
ideas for simple curtains and shades

Lucinda Ganderton and Ali Watkinson
with photography by Polly Eltes

RYLAND
PETERS
& SMALL

LONDON NEW YORK

**Designer** Fiona Walker
**Junior designer** Sarah Walden
**Senior editor** Sophie Bevan
**Location research manager** Kate Brunt
**Picture and location research** Emily Westlake
**Production** Patricia Harrington
**Art director** Gabriella Le Grazie
**Publishing director** Alison Starling

**Illustrator** Lizzie Sanders

First published in the USA in 2002
by Ryland Peters & Small, Inc
519 Broadway, 5th Floor
New York, NY10012
www.rylandpeters.com

10 9 8 7 6 5 4 3 2 1

**Important note:** the imperial-metric conversions
supplied in this book are not exact, and have been
adapted to suit the requirements of each project.
Always follow either the imperial or the metric
measurements when making up a project.

Library of Congress Cataloging-in-
Publication Data

Ganderton, Lucinda.
    Window Treatments : a source book of
contemporary ideas for simple curtains and
shades / Lucinda Ganderton & Ali Watkinson
; with photography by Polly Eltes.
        p. cm.
        Includes index.
    ISBN 1 84172 329 0
    1. Draperies. 2. Window shades.
I. Watkinson, Ali. II. Title.

TT390 .G35 2002
747'.3–dc21                    2002066755

Printed and bound in China

# contents

# introduction

At the risk of sounding dramatic, there has been nothing short of a revolution in curtain style over the last few years. While it's not exactly curtains for curtains yet, the former rule that window dressings should be heavily gathered, lined and interlined, hung from elaborate tracks or poles, festooned with valances and tiebacks, and, in consequence, heinously expensive, has been blown asunder.

A relaxed, contemporary approach now prevails that, quite rightly, questions whether curtains need be gathered at all when a flat panel might do the same job; or whether ugly tracks can be replaced with discreet tension wire. This isn't to say that traditional curtains no longer have a place, just that you might want to reserve them for more formal situations or make them from inexpensive muslin, ticking, or burlap rather than damasks, velvets, and silks.

There are still some considerations to bear in mind if you are to make the most of your windows and, consequently, of the room as a whole. The first concerns the primary purpose of your window treatment. How much natural daylight are you prepared to give up? Do you want to maximize or minimize the view, keep the room warm, or simply preserve your privacy? Second, assess the merits of your window. If it's a thing of beauty, endeavor to show it off. If it's somewhat lacking, and many are, consider a style that will disguise its defects. Finally, bear in mind the function of the room. A style appropriate for a formal living room would probably be impractical in a steamy kitchen, and vice versa. Common sense and lateral thinking will guide you, and may throw up some witty reinterpretations. Bathroom windows might be dressed with practical shower-curtain fabric, while in the bedroom, cozy wool blankets can be held up with sturdy clips. The nearest there is to a rule is that anything goes.

**opposite** In this contemporary bedroom, stylish cream damask fabric has been given an informal, ungathered heading. Chic and unfussy, it has the advantage of requiring less fabric than more traditional styles. The twig "valance" adds a witty, natural flourish.

**this page** Recently, fabrics in natural fibers and colors have come to the fore, but as these examples show, they need not result in plain or boring window treatments. A velvet ribbon trim combined with a triple pleat heading lifts neutral linen curtains above the ordinary. Stunning white-on-white hand-embroidered linen is shown to great advantage in otherwise plain Roman shades. And unusually proportioned vertical stripes lend a crisply tailored look to blinds at a bay window.

# styles

SELECTING FABRICS

WORKING WITH PROPORTIONS

SHEERS

DETAILS

# SELECTING FABRICS

The enormous variety of fabrics now available can be mind-bogglingly confusing. However, by imposing some practical limitations, you can begin to narrow the field.

Start with the purpose of the room. Is its use predominantly formal or informal? This may influence whether you choose a chic or inexpensive fabric, although even cheap, utilitarian fabrics can look impressive when bedecked with opulent trimmings. Will you need to wash the curtains? This is especially important in kitchens, bathrooms, and children's bedrooms—drycleaning curtains can be prohibitively expensive.

Then consider the physical characteristics of the room. Is it sunny or dark? If it's the latter, heavy, dark-colored fabrics will tend to rob the room of what little light it has, so are best avoided. Is it a cold or warm room? A cozy, richly colored fabric will warm up a cold room both visually and physically.

Think, too, about your preferred style of window treatment. If you want the fabric to gather in sumptuous folds, choose a medium- to heavyweight material, since lighter fabrics will be too flimsy to hang well. Conversely, light- to medium-weight fabrics make better shades, since heavy fabrics are often too bulky to fold neatly. Other factors to take into account are the period of the room, which could be highlighted with a fabric of that era, and its size—small rooms are easily overpowered by large-patterned fabrics.

Finally, bear in mind that curtain fabrics do not have to be purpose-made. As long as you take adequate precautions regarding fire retardancy, dressmaking fabrics such as sari lengths and suiting cloth, or recycled furnishings such as linen sheets and dishtowels, may be cheaper, and more interesting, alternatives.

**opposite, above left** Utilitarian ticking offers a cheery, cheap, and practically indestructible choice, whether you track down densely woven period examples—which are salvaged from old mattresses—or use one of the many modern interpretations.

**opposite, above right** Recycling antique bed and table linen into curtain fabric allows you to make a feature of its wonderful soft drape and eggshell sheen, the result of many years of careful laundering.

**opposite, below left** Even simple coarse-weave fabrics make undeniably glamorous curtains when teamed with sumptuous velvet ribbons and a shiny silk lining.

**opposite, below right** Dressmaking materials like these Indian sari lengths can make inspiring fabric choices, with unusual features like embroidered hems rethought to create decorative leading edges.

**this page** Fabrics needn't be brightly colored and ornately patterned to be eye-catching: this fine, self-colored paisley print needs little more than a delicate beaded trim to make it work.

# plain colors
## and weaves

Attaching the adjective "plain" to anything can sound like a criticism, with the synonyms "dull" and "boring" (and the implied accusation of a sartorial copout) never far away. But plain—solid—fabrics are anything but boring. Think of a swathe of brightly colored silk and how light plays across its folds, or of a time-worn expanse of rough linen and the charming irregularity of its weave. Both have a character and individuality that are far from dull.

Indeed, the dyes used, the way a solid-colored yarn is woven, and the treatments applied to the finished fabric can create amazing variations of subtle pattern. Herringbone, seersucker, bouclé, moiré, and chintz are just a few of the disparate "plains."

Select a plain fabric the way you would choose a paint color for the walls. If you want the effect to be advancing and dominating, choose a bold color that contrasts with the rest of the room. For a softer, receding effect, ideal to enhance the sense of space in a small or dark room, choose a pale shade that matches or tones with the other elements.

Where the window dressings will be a prominent and potentially dominant feature in a room (more than likely requiring lots of

**opposite, above right** Here a voile curtain in subtle contrasting bands of soft cream is anchored with a border of heavier silk with woven stripes.

**opposite, below left** This ivory silk satin positively shimmers in the light, bringing texture and interest to its heavy folds.

**opposite, below right** A bright yellow curtain is far from dull, and the acid tones of the fabric are softened by the embossed interwoven pattern.

**this page** Plain fabrics make effective layered window treatments. Here floaty voile curtains with a matching valance are teamed with a cotton shade to provide varying degrees of privacy. The torchon lace edging adds to the feminine effect.

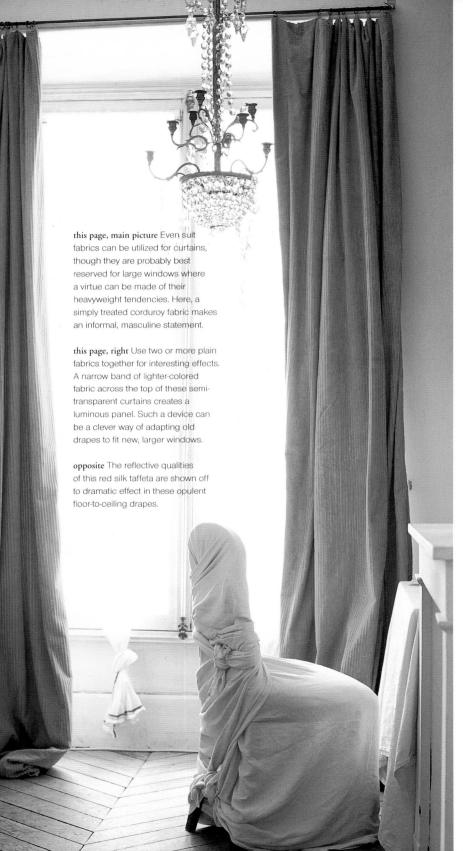

**this page, main picture** Even suit fabrics can be utilized for curtains, though they are probably best reserved for large windows where a virtue can be made of their heavyweight tendencies. Here, a simply treated corduroy fabric makes an informal, masculine statement.

**this page, right** Use two or more plain fabrics together for interesting effects. A narrow band of lighter-colored fabric across the top of these semi-transparent curtains creates a luminous panel. Such a device can be a clever way of adapting old drapes to fit new, larger windows.

**opposite** The reflective qualities of this red silk taffeta are shown off to dramatic effect in these opulent floor-to-ceiling drapes.

fabric), choosing a plain, solid-colored material can be a sensible, exciting—and flexible—option. Used unembellished, plain curtains and shades have a stark, structural quality. Think of the way a simple block of color, whether it is on a wall or canvas or a throw, stands out from its surroundings. Yet, with the simple addition of trimmings, appliqué, or decorative tiebacks, they can metamorphose into any number of different styles, from masculine to feminine, flouncy to tailored, pretty to city-slick. And should you want to use any of these decorative effects, a plain fabric will act as a flattering backdrop, highlighting rather than hiding their details.

Aside from their individual adaptability, solid-colored curtains and shades are also usefully flexible partners in an interior scheme as a whole, allowing inexpensive and easily revamped accessories like pillows and throws to dictate the style as the mood takes you. So if it's likely that your tastes or the function of the room will alter (the former is pretty much a dead cert), and if you're investing serious sums, then playing safe is actually a canny option.

**left** Teaming two mismatched checks can work well if the color match is spot-on. Narrow red braid stitched over the seams stops the confluence of the patterns from looking messy.

**above** The striped curtains and plaid blanket make natural partners, united by their predominant color.

**opposite, left** Edging the hem of this valance prevents the feature from getting lost in the bold pattern.

**opposite, center** Ticking, traditionally white with a colored stripe, now comes in multicolored examples that are perfect for tailored Roman shades.

**opposite, right** A courageous pairing of a plaid and check works because the yellows are a perfect match.

# geometric patterns

Whether woven or printed, stripes and checks are the most prolific of geometric patterns, coming as they do in almost every combination of color and scale. Their applications are endless; indeed, you only have to contrast the humble ticking with a stylish Regency stripe, or a fresh-faced gingham with a bold checkerboard to get an idea of their versatility. Used together, in coordinating proportions and colors, stripes and checks have a natural affinity that makes them a designer favorite—but introduce textural variations into the room if you don't want the results to look too formulaic.

Small checks can bring structure and order to an otherwise busy scheme, and team particularly well with toile de Jouy and floral patterns, but stick to coordinating colors. As in fashion, though perhaps with more flattering results, stripes can be used to mislead the eye. So horizontal stripes can disguise an overly narrow window by creating the illusion of width, while vertical stripes can be used to correct an over-wide window.

Besides stripes and checks, and the cheeriest of geometrics—spots—other options are as varied as the windows that need dressing. When using a multicolored geometric, such as a plaid, team it with solid fabrics in the predominant color, or, if you want to go for saturation, more of the same, but think very carefully before introducing other patterns into the mix. Use fashion-led abstract geometrics with caution since they can easily become dated—good news if you love a particular era, but bad if that style passes out of favor. And, if you are making the window treatments yourself, be extra careful with geometrics—any mismatched seams or wonky hems will be more obvious than with a plain or abstract-patterned fabric.

**this page** Combining pictorial fabrics can be very successful when, as in this Arabian-style canopied room, their colors match exactly and rely on coordinating motifs.

**opposite, above** Bobble fringe along the leading edge and hem of these toile de Jouy drapes gives structure to the large scale and relative randomness of the pattern. Using red instead of the more obvious navy blue for the trim adds a frivolous touch.

**opposite, below left** The large floral sprigs on this printed voile are prettily highlighted by the light from the window.

**opposite, below center** Small checks in a matching color sit easily with this floral and stripe print, while a contrasting edging in the predominant color draws attention to the unusual scalloped valance.

**opposite, below right** Leaving this floral sheer lightly gathered allows the design to be fully appreciated.

# florals
## and pictorials

From over-the-top chintzes to history-invoking toile de Jouys, from elegant paisleys to winsome nursery prints, florals and pictorials have the capacity to be both completely charming and completely overwhelming.

If you're using a large-patterned fabric, then you're necessarily going to be making a big statement. Can the window and room handle the design? Will you be able to see enough of the pattern to do it justice? Will you (or in the case of nursery prints, your children) still love the design in a few years' time? As with multicolored geometrics, these fabrics will not easily share room space with other patterns and are best teamed with solid fabrics, small checks, or narrow stripes. Unless, that is, you make your selection from one of the fabric lines offering coordinating florals or pictorials. Relying on both a color and motif theme to unite them, these pairings are best used in unequal proportions to allow one design to dominate. Large-scale patterns will also benefit greatly from grounding with plain edgings or trimmings that pick up the main color.

By contrast, smaller-scale patterns take on an unobtrusive regularity, with the true nature of their design being lost when they are used en masse or seen from a distance, as they would be in a larger room. To do justice to the intricacy of these designs, confine them to more diminutive windows and smaller rooms.

this page By using minimalist hoops and clips on this panel of traditional-style printed velvet, the luxurious look easily adapts to a modern setting.

opposite, above left Expensive fabrics needn't be used en masse to steal the show. Here floral brocade, used as a border, transforms this ribbed shade.

opposite, above center Velvet isn't ideal for shades, unless, as here, the window is large enough to give the fabric room to pleat neatly.

opposite, above right A London shade makes a flamboyant treatment in a fine damask. The modest quantity of fabric this style of shade uses makes this a relatively inexpensive way to use a luxurious fabric. Note how the narrow edging defines the characteristic outline of the shade.

opposite, below Theatrical and sumptuous, these peach velvet curtains with heavy fringed swags make a dramatic focal point in this understated room scheme.

# wools, velvets, and damasks

Resolutely at the luxurious end of the fabric spectrum, not least because of their cost, wool, velvet, and damask add instant glamour, warmth, and a sense of tradition to a room. As such, they are best employed where comfort and stylishness are required—living rooms, halls, and bedrooms being the most obvious contenders. The weight of these fabrics (and their consequent drape-ability) means that, budget allowing, they will make beautiful, heavily gathered, full-length draperies. To play on their opulent nature, add extravagant trimmings and tiebacks and ornate poles to create a really sumptuous, theatrical effect.

While these fabrics are expensive, they can reasonably be considered a good investment because they will never go out of date. That said, they needn't look entirely traditional or be reserved solely for period interiors. Modern reinterpretations of wool fabrics, for instance, have led to vintage blankets being transformed into "instant" curtains. Meanwhile, tweeds and suit fabrics can be used to add a witty, tailored look to a masculine room. Both would look equally at home in an urban loft or a "country" home.

On a practical note, all curtains made from these heavier fabrics should be lined to give body and to protect them from the ravages of sunlight, which can both fade and destroy natural fibers. Interlining (a third layer sandwiched between the main fabric and lining) will improve the drape of large, traditional curtains, while effectively keeping any drafts at bay.

# sheer fabrics

No longer banished to a secondary role hiding behind heavier-weight curtains, sheers have been embraced for their simplicity and ethereal appearance and are, more likely than not, used alone in today's centrally heated and double-glazed homes. In consequence, there has never been a greater choice of natural sheer fabrics available, in both plain and decorative styles.

The cheapest of these is plain cotton voile, which creates a very soft, simple effect and is ideal for working rooms like kitchens and bathrooms, where curtains need frequent laundering. Other sheer fabrics include the more showy silk organzas and voiles, with their beautiful sheen, and delicate laces which, removed from their traditional fusty settings, can look surprisingly fresh and pretty. However, with generous natural light, any lightweight, loosely woven fabric will take on a degree of transparency.

The range of decorative sheers is increasing all the time. Embellishments include appliquéd shapes, beads, sequins, tiny mirrors, and embroidery, as well as cutout and dévoré work. It is also easy to add embellishment to plain sheers yourself, should you decide they need livening up. Other options include the many sheer fabrics designed for dressmaking—while they may not be tough enough to withstand constant handling or the long-term effects of sunlight that window treatments are subjected to, it may be reasonable to take the view that they don't actually need to last forever.

Colored sheers can look amazing, although it is worth trying out a sample of fabric at the window before committing yourself, because the effect can alter dramatically depending on the quality of light behind them, and can also radically affect the carefully considered color scheme of your room. As an inexpensive tryout, consider giving any old sheers, that are looking less than pristine, a new lease on life by dyeing them.

The new generation of double-width fabrics—available in widths of up to 3 yards—is ideal for making sheer curtains. Used sideways with their width as the drop, they mean very large curtains can be made without the need for seams, which not only saves work, but looks better, too. These are a particular boon, given the current craze for living in open-plan, industrial-type spaces where over-scale curtains and dividers, particularly sheer ones that preserve the architecture and sense of space, come into their own.

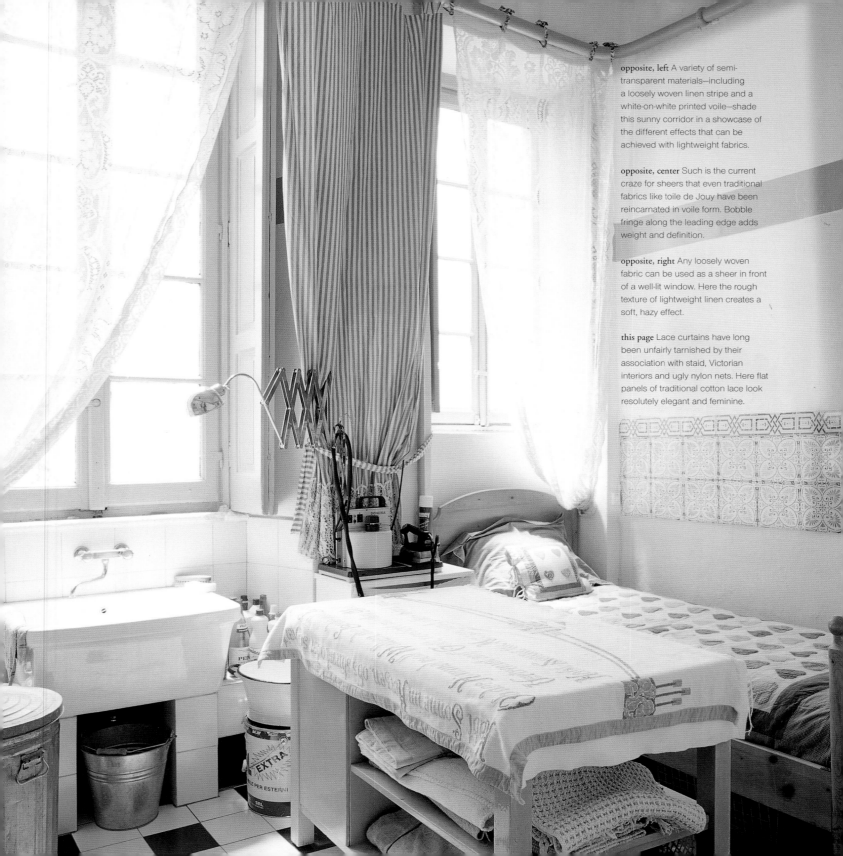

**opposite, left** A variety of semi-transparent materials—including a loosely woven linen stripe and a white-on-white printed voile—shade this sunny corridor in a showcase of the different effects that can be achieved with lightweight fabrics.

**opposite, center** Such is the current craze for sheers that even traditional fabrics like toile de Jouy have been reincarnated in voile form. Bobble fringe along the leading edge adds weight and definition.

**opposite, right** Any loosely woven fabric can be used as a sheer in front of a well-lit window. Here the rough texture of lightweight linen creates a soft, hazy effect.

**this page** Lace curtains have long been unfairly tarnished by their association with staid, Victorian interiors and ugly nylon nets. Here flat panels of traditional cotton lace look resolutely elegant and feminine.

# WORKING WITH PROPORTIONS

Few homeowners are blessed with beautifully proportioned floor-to-ceiling sash or groovy 1930s metal windows—at least, not at the moment they become the height of desirability. Most of us inherit the sort of ill-thought-out features that result from shortsighted cost-cutting, poor design, and years of inappropriate renovations.

Consequently, when devising window treatments, it's often a case of cursing the architect, builder, or do-it-yourselfer who created the too small, too narrow, or lopsided window you actually have and making the best of a bad job. With a keen eye, it's amazing what visual tricks can be pulled to rectify the imperfect shape or proportion of a window or even the awkward way it is set within the wall. Often these ruses will require a degree of interpretation because no two situations will be quite the same. Draw your window to scale on graph paper and sketch your ideas for curtains or a shade to gauge how the approach works in principle. Bear in mind that the window treatment will look very different when the curtains are closed or the shade is down.

**opposite, above left** Leaving the wall behind the radiator unpapered and using a fabric that matches the paint color adds length to this window.

**opposite, above right** Lightweight shutters that sit within the window frame preserve the architectural proportions of an attractive window.

**opposite, below left** At first glance, these two windows appear to match, but the one on the left is actually gently curved. The clever use of three Roman shades maintains the horizontal symmetry and disguises the differences.

**opposite, below right** Café curtains are the answer to many awkward window shapes. They should align with the central sash for best results.

**this page** Modern shades are amazingly flexible and, taking up very little space when retracted, are especially useful in situations with no room for curtains to be pulled open at the side of the window.

# wide windows

Wide windows aren't necessarily a problem—they look great in an Art Deco apartment, for instance, where they should be emphasized to the full. However, as Federal architects (and the classical scholars who inspired them) knew, the eye is best pleased where the proportions of the feature or building observed replicate ideal geometric shapes such as the square, circle, cube, or cube-and-a-half. The greater the deviation from this ideal, the less attractive the feature appears.

Happily, there are ways to restore this balance. Overly wide windows can be visually divided by using several pairs of curtains, so one large window is depicted as several smaller ones. This approach can work particularly well where the window stretches the full width of the wall, leaving little room to accommodate the bulk of wide curtains when they are open. It has the disadvantage of significantly reducing the amount of light the room enjoys, which may be a sacrifice worth making if the light in the room is too bright, but to reduce the loss and minimize bulk, use a lightly gathered, light- to medium-weight fabric, or opt for a series of shades or blinds instead (from a practical point of view, it would be impossible to make a single shade to span a large area).

Where there is space between the ceiling and the top of the window, another way to disguise excessive width is to exaggerate the apparent height of the window by

Here an inappropriate modern window in a period house has been cunningly disguised with the use of an elaborate valance built to look as if it is part of the architecture. Allowing the extra-long curtains to overlap the window narrows the width, helping to disguise the shape further. A semi-translucent shade allows light in while blotting out the ugly carpentry.

raising the track or pole to just below the ceiling and hanging floor-length, or longer, drapes. Any unsightly void could be covered by a valance.

Partnering curtains with sheer panels or shades to create a layered effect will also obscure the unrelenting horizontal character of a wide window. And, of course, a fabric patterned with vertical stripes—even a subtle self-stripe would do the trick—is a classic disguise when making treatments for wide windows. The wider the window is, the wider the stripes should be, but you needn't restrict your choice to ready-made striped fabrics. Have fun mixing and matching bands of different fabrics to create an

individual design (which can also be a good way of using up remnants), varying the widths of the panels to make the effect easier on the eye. The execution will need to be perfect, especially where flat panels or shades are being used, since they will offer up any wonky seams for immediate scrutiny. Use ribbons and braids over seams to hide any minor imperfections in the stitching and to accentuate the vertical bands. Another variation on this theme would be to use loose contrasting lengths of ribbon or braid as long decorative ties for curtain headings or as hold-ups for unstructured pleated and rolled Swedish shades. These will, again, help visually to break up the width.

**below far left** A shade made from two harmonizing silk fabrics (which are also used in the matching padded valance) shows that with careful measuring and making, a "homemade" stripe can create a dramatic effect. Here the decorative trimming serves to hide the seams and to further highlight the vertical bands.

**below center** Floor-to-ceiling drapes in a subtle self-stripe fabric soften the dominating effect of these vast picture windows in a city skyscraper by reducing the apparent width. The curtain track is mounted on the ceiling to make use of every inch of available height.

**below right** Something as simple as using a contrasting color for the ties in these pleated shades adds vertical demarcation and breaks up the width of these wide, shallow windows. Since these shades are designed to be left partially unfurled to obscure the view, they consequently mask some of the available light, so they are unlined and made with a lightweight, loosely woven fabric.

**above** This trio of blinds has been tailored to match the window architecture and allow the side windows to be open while still maintaining privacy in the bathroom.

**far left** Although a single curtain rod has been installed across this run of recessed sashes, individual sill-length curtains in a transparent material allow the window architecture to predominate.

**left** This wide window in an Art Deco apartment suits the scale of the room and is enhanced and celebrated by the horizontal "skeleton" of a semi-transparent Roman shade.

# no-sew sheet curtains

Antique linen has a unique quality that only comes after years of use and laundering. Monogrammed sheets, hand towels, and lace-edged tablecloths can be found at textile auctions, specialized outlets, or flea markets. They can then easily be adapted as curtains and, if decorative clips are used to hang them on a metal rod or wire, require no sewing.

**MATERIALS AND EQUIPMENT**
sheet
tailor's chalk
curtain clips

**MEASURING**
The valance should be between ⅛ and ¼ the height of the window, but the exact depth will depend on the size of the cloth and the shape of the window.

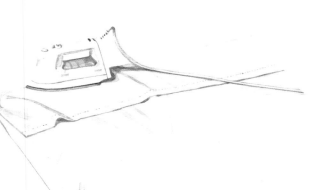

**VARIATION**
Embroidered hand towels (left) have been made into half-curtains with simple clips. Sunlight filters through the eyelet work to give a warm translucency to the starched linen.

**2** Using tailor's chalk, mark a point at each top corner. Draw a series of equally spaced points between them, one for each curtain clip.

**1** Wash the sheet at a high temperature to remove any marks or crease lines, and iron it well to restore its original appearance. Turn the top edge forward to form a valance and press along the fold.

**3** Put the clips in place and hang the curtain from the pole.

# tall windows

When dealing with tall, narrow windows, you need simply to reverse the approach taken for wide windows. Sill-length curtains are often the best choice. They will help by effectively truncating the perceived length of the window, whereas floor-length drapes will necessarily have the opposite effect, drawing attention to the vertical height.

Where floor-length curtains are required, you can increase the apparent width of the window by extending the pole or track well beyond the edges of the frame. This will create the illusion of a much wider feature and can be especially effective where the tall window is marooned in a large expanse of wall. If you do take this option, be mindful that when the curtains are open, they will need to have enough body to fill this extra housing or wall space comfortably.

If you can afford to cut down on the available light in the room, another trick would be to reduce the apparent height of the overly tall window by setting a deep valance as close to the top of the window frame as possible, which will have the effect of bisecting the window.

The classic cosmetic disguise is to employ horizontal bands, either in the form of a striped fabric or a curtain or shade made of several different horizontal panels. Also consider attaching a deep border in a contrasting color to solid-colored floor-length curtains (roughly one-third of the height of the overall curtain in

**below** Here a plain metal curtain pole has been suspended from a ceiling beam which, together with the extra-long curtains spilling onto the floor, creates the illusion that this truncated narrow window is really a more attractive floor-to-ceiling version.

**right** Used with restraint, an ornamental heading will subtly draw attention. The tasseled pennants that bisect the top of these plain curtains draw the eye above the top of the frame to the classical reeded pole. The pole itself extends beyond the width of the window to add importance to this modestly sized living-room window.

**far right** The large-scale checks of this woven fabric echo the grid created by the heavy glazing bars of a balconied window overlooking a city square. The curtains have been left unlined to maximize the amount of light that enters the room.

depth), which will draw the eye down, making the curtain appear shorter than it is. Similarly, an integral valance (again, roughly one-third the height of the overall curtain in depth) in a contrasting, lighter color will break up the vertical length.

A simple sill-length café curtain that neatly bisects the window or a shade constructed from a carefully chosen fabric—again, the obvious being a horizontal stripe or several different horizontal panels—eradicate the awkwardness of tall windows that stop short of the floor, an aspect that floor-length drapes would tend to draw attention to. Shades are particularly useful for tall windows where the frame extends right up to the ceiling, preventing a pole or track from being mounted on the outside of the frame.

# tie-top bordered curtain

Natural cotton, which hangs in soft folds, lends itself to this informal tied heading. The curtain is folded into a series of deep pleats without any reinforcement and is given extra weight by the deep border of unbleached linen. The seam is embellished with row of herringbone stitch. If you are making the curtain from a lighter fabric, or to cover a smaller window than the one shown here, you should reduce the size of the pleats accordingly.

MATERIALS AND EQUIPMENT
unbleached linen
cream cotton fabric
matching sewing thread
small safety pin
cream embroidery thread
basic sewing kit

MEASURING
A = length of curtain pole
B = from bottom of curtain rings to floor

TO CALCULATE THE NUMBER OF PLEATS
The pleats are at 4-in (10-cm) intervals and each one takes up 8 in (20 cm) of fabric. Divide A by 10 and subtract 1 to find the number required.

CUTTING OUT
*main curtain:*
width = number of pleats x 12 in (30 cm) plus 2 in (6 cm)
length = ¾ B plus 2 in (6 cm)

*border:*
width = number of pleats x 12 in (30 cm) plus 2 in (6 cm)
length = ¼ B plus 2 in (6 cm)

*ties:*
Cut one for each pleat
width = 2 in (6 cm)
length = 12 in (30 cm)

**1** Pin and baste the border to the bottom of the main curtain. Machine stitch ½ in (1.5 cm) from the edge and press the seam open.

**2** Press under a ½ in (1.5 cm) double hem along each side of the curtain. Pin and baste, then machine stitch.

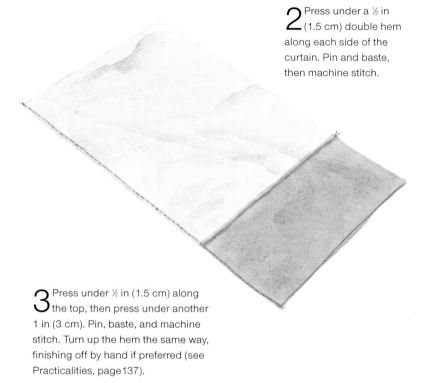

**3** Press under ½ in (1.5 cm) along the top, then press under another 1 in (3 cm). Pin, baste, and machine stitch. Turn up the hem the same way, finishing off by hand if preferred (see Practicalities, page 137).

4 To make each tie, fold a strip in half lengthwise. Pin and baste the long edges together and machine stitch, leaving a ¼ in (5 mm) seam allowance. Fasten a safety pin to one open end. Feed the pin back through the fabric tube to turn it the right way out. Unpin, then press flat so the seam lies along one side. Turn under ¼ in (5 mm) to finish the raw edges and close with slipstitch. Press in half.

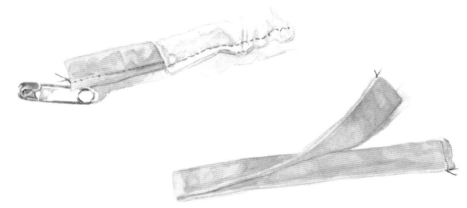

5 To mark the positions of the pleats: insert a pin 6 in (15 cm) from each corner of the top edge; place a row of pins at approximately 12 in (30 cm) intervals; mark a point 4 in (10 cm) on each side of each pin using tailor's chalk.

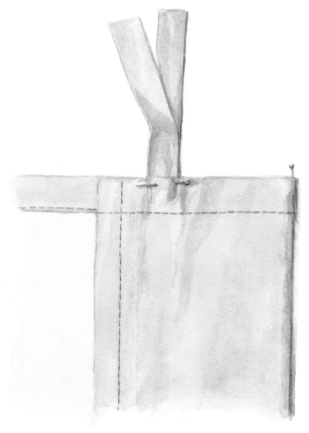

6 Starting at the left corner and working from the right side of the fabric, pin and baste ⅝ in (1.5 cm) of the folded end of a tie between the first and second chalk marks. Remove the marker pin, which now lies at the center front of the pleat.

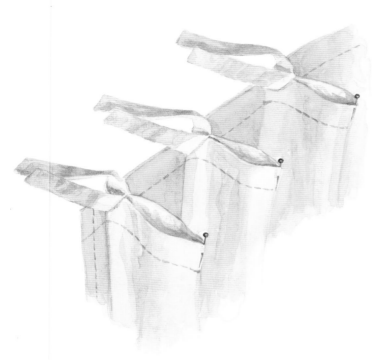

7 Attach the other ties, placing each one between two chalk marks, leaving 4 in (10 cm) of fabric between each pleat. Machine stitch across the bottom of the ties ¼ in (5 mm) from the top of the curtain. Work a few reverse stitches at each end to strengthen the row.

8 Finish by working a row of herringbone stitch (see Practicalities, page 137) over the seam between the curtain and the border.

9 Knot each tie securely to a curtain ring in order to hang the curtain.

**top row, left** Unlined tab-top curtains provide a simple treatment and, being insubstantial, leave the window relatively unobscured when open.

**top row, center** These tightly gathered lightweight cotton curtains are full enough to be decorative and not too skimpy, yet not so heavy as to obscure the window.

**top row, right** The pole for these floor-to-eave curtains is ingeniously suspended between two rafters.

**bottom row, left** A tray cloth makes an easy café curtain at this diminutive sash and offers privacy during the day.

**bottom row, center** Most large-scale patterns are wasted over a small area, except for airy, random designs like this embroidered sheer.

**bottom row, right** To make the curtains floor or sill length is a dilemma with small windows. This solution, twisting the bulk of the fabric over a holdback, is good compromise.

# small windows

With small windows, where insulation is unlikely to be much of a problem, it may be that you can do without curtains or shades altogether and merely enjoy portholelike glimpses of the outside world. Where a window treatment is necessary, any loss of light will be keenly felt, so a design that does not obscure the glass will be required.

All the techniques for disguising wide or tall windows can be applied to small windows, although they will have to be adapted to suit the more diminutive proportions. So, for example, use pinstripes rather than ordinary stripes, horizontally or vertically, to broaden or narrow as required. Avoid large-scale patterned fabrics altogether, except for a medium-sized window, where an airy, abstract design can help disguise a boxy shape.

Whether floor-length curtains will work depends largely on how high or low the window is positioned in the wall—too far either way and they will look ridiculous.

Where there is little room to pull the curtains back, use only very lightweight fabrics that will gather and hang comfortably in a confined space. Consider, too, reducing the amount of fabric used by applying a smaller ratio of fabric widths than normal or by cutting back to a simple panel. Low-key headings, such as ties or curtain clips, will probably work best in these instances.

For recessed attic or dormer windows, where a normal treatment would obscure the light, sill-length curtains hung from portière rods that open out like shutters offer a nifty solution. For

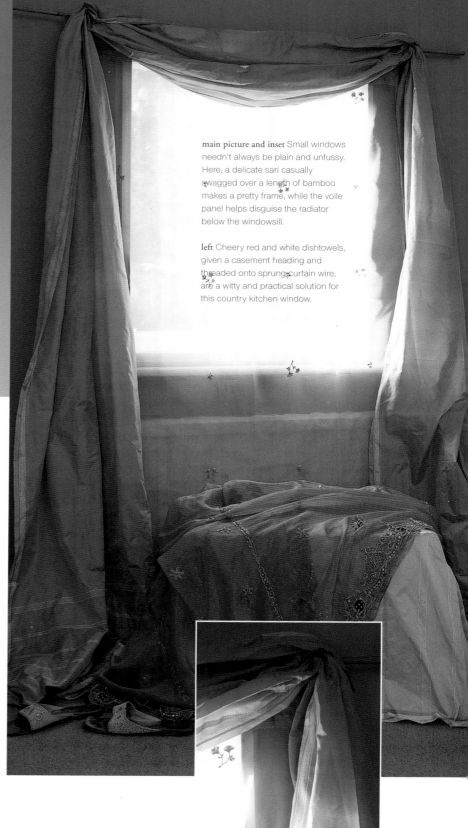

**main picture and inset** Small windows needn't always be plain and unfussy. Here, a delicate sari casually swagged over a length of bamboo makes a pretty frame, while the voile panel helps disguise the radiator below the windowsill.

**left** Cheery red and white dishtowels, given a casement heading and threaded onto sprung curtain wire, are a witty and practical solution for this country kitchen window.

a more tailored, minimal look, use roll-up or Swedish shades, which take up less space when retracted than Roman or (heaven forbid!) balloon shades, or hang the latter styles outside of the window frame or recess to minimize the loss of light.

Where privacy is required or an unattractive view needs to be hidden, consider whether a sheer might not be sufficient alone, because a layered treatment could look fussy and heavy. For an even cleaner solution, a half sheer hung at the same height as the central sash might preserve modesty and satisfy aesthetic ideals while still allowing plenty of precious light into the room.

One way in which small windows surpass all others is in their modest fabric requirements. They offer the perfect opportunity to use up leftover fabrics or, less frugally, to select the most desirable fabrics that would be too expensive for larger projects. They also make the perfect recipient for carefully hoarded pieces of antique bed and table linen, which are rarely used today for their original purpose.

# double-sided dormer curtain

A hinged portière rod that swings out to lie flat against the adjacent wall during the day is the ideal solution for a small dormer window. Both the front and back of the curtain will be visible at different times, so they should be equally attractive. This reversible panel is made from solid fabric with a woven border, backed and piped with coordinating gingham. The method can be simplified by leaving out the piping (skip steps 1–3).

MATERIALS AND EQUIPMENT
main fabric
backing fabric
fine piping cord
matching sewing thread
yardstick
portière rod to fit width of window frame
drill, screwdriver, and screws
basic sewing kit

MEASURING
A = length of portière rod
B = from 1½ in (4 cm) above top of portière rod to sill

CUTTING OUT
front and back alike
width = A plus 4 in (10 cm) for seams and fullness
length = B plus 1½ in (4 cm) for seams

PIPING CORD
length = 2A + 2B plus 12 in (30 cm)

1 Cut a 2-in (5-cm) wide strip of gingham to cover the piping cord. Join pieces as necessary to reach the required length and press the seams open. Fold the strip over the cord with the right side out and pin, then baste in place close to the cord.

2 Starting 2–4 in (5–10 cm) from one top corner and leaving a 1½ in (4 cm) loose end, pin the piping around the right side of the front panel, matching the raw edges. Clip into the seam allowance at the corners. Baste down, leaving a 1½ in (4 cm) overlap.

3 Take out the basting for 1½ in (4 cm) at each end of the piping. Trim the cord so the two ends butt up and stitch them together loosely. Press ½ in (1 cm) under at the end of one strip. Fold it over the other strip and baste through all the layers. Put a zipper foot on the machine and stitch down ⅛ in (3 mm) from the cord all around the panel.

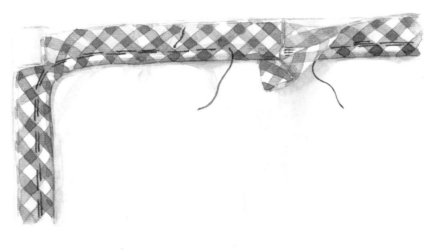

4 With right sides together, pin and baste the front and back panels. If you are using piping, it will be sandwiched between the two pieces of fabric (as shown, right).

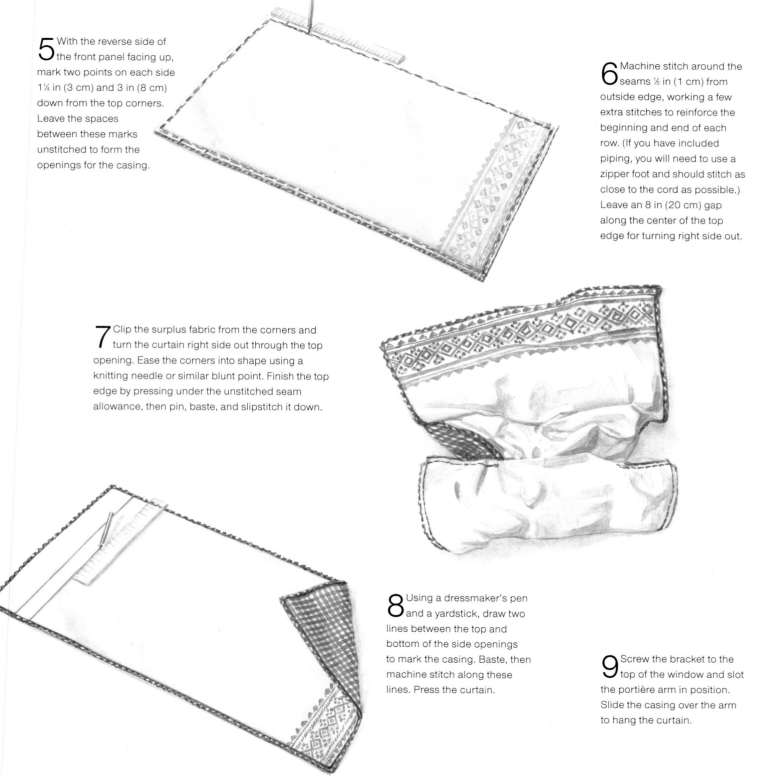

**5** With the reverse side of the front panel facing up, mark two points on each side 1¼ in (3 cm) and 3 in (8 cm) down from the top corners. Leave the spaces between these marks unstitched to form the openings for the casing.

**6** Machine stitch around the seams ½ in (1 cm) from outside edge, working a few extra stitches to reinforce the beginning and end of each row. (If you have included piping, you will need to use a zipper foot and should stitch as close to the cord as possible.) Leave an 8 in (20 cm) gap along the center of the top edge for turning right side out.

**7** Clip the surplus fabric from the corners and turn the curtain right side out through the top opening. Ease the corners into shape using a knitting needle or similar blunt point. Finish the top edge by pressing under the unstitched seam allowance, then pin, baste, and slipstitch it down.

**8** Using a dressmaker's pen and a yardstick, draw two lines between the top and bottom of the side openings to mark the casing. Baste, then machine stitch along these lines. Press the curtain.

**9** Screw the bracket to the top of the window and slot the portière arm in position. Slide the casing over the arm to hang the curtain.

# patchwork panel

Collect fragments of antique fabrics to make this patchwork kitchen curtain. Delicate white cottons—embroidered lawn, drawn-thread work, and eyelet lace—work particularly well against a window. The panel is edged with lace and hung from a narrow white rod with a row of checked ribbon loops. This project is very individual and can be adapted to suit whatever interesting pieces of fabric and edgings you can find—the result will be unique.

MATERIALS AND EQUIPMENT
embroidered fabric
gingham
checked ribbon
cotton lace
matching sewing thread
basic sewing kit

MEASURING
width = length of curtain rod plus 4 in (10 cm) for fullness
length = from 2 in (5 cm) below pole to 2 in (5 cm) above sill

**1** Wash and press all the fabric. Cut out a selection of strips and rectangles, discarding any worn areas.

**2** Lay the fabric pieces on the floor, taking time to create a balanced arrangement. Add an extra ½ in (1.5 cm) around each piece for seam allowances when calculating the required width and length.

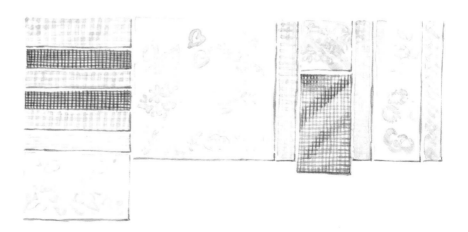

3 Join all the horizontal seams first, using a narrow French seam. With wrong sides together, pin and baste two pieces. Machine stitch ¼ in (7 mm) from the edge. Trim the seam allowance to ⅛ in (3 mm) and refold so that the right sides are facing. Stitch again, ¼ in (7 mm) from the fold. Press the seam to one side.

4 Join the vertical seams in the same way, then trim the sides of the panel, if necessary, so they are straight.

5 Press under ½ in (1.5 cm) around all four sides. Fold the edges up to the crease and press again to make a narrow double hem. Baste and machine stitch down.

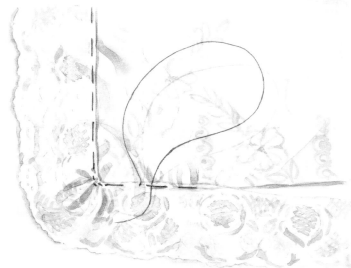

6 Baste a length of lace around the panel, gathering it slightly as you go to fit around the corners. Slipstitch the two ends together, then machine stitch close to the edge.

7 The loops are made from 5-in (12-cm) lengths of ribbon. Press under ½ in (1.5 cm) at each end and slipstitch together along the folds. Pin along the wrong side of the top edge at intervals of approximately 6 in (15 cm). Slipstitch in place and hang from the rod.

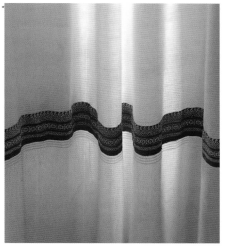

# bays, recesses, and
# awkward shapes

Ironically, it is often the most interesting and attractive windows that are the most difficult to devise window treatments for, with arched and round windows being obvious examples. Indeed, their very attractiveness begs the question: is it really necessary to disguise them with curtains or shades at all? But where it can't be avoided, there are several ways in which their merits can be preserved, the most obvious solution being to extend the track well beyond the frame or recess so the curtain can be pulled well clear. The disadvantage with this is that the window is hidden completely when the curtains are closed.

The graceful sweep of an arched window, in particular, can be maintained and further emphasized by using curtains with a stationary heading that replicates the curve by means of a flexible track. They have the disadvantage of reducing the light coming into the room and, perhaps, look a little fussy in today's pared-down interiors. A more minimal solution would be to use a half, café-style curtain to screen the lower portion of the window while leaving the

**opposite** Here, individual shades, in unobtrusive plain white fabric that blends with the paintwork, provide necessary screening without detracting from the leaded windows or the owner's unusual decorative flourishes.

**this page** A vintage bolt of fabric featuring an attractive braided border has been ingeniously used to make coordinated Roman shades at a bay window. To have used curtains in this situation—with such a beautiful frame and molding—would have been sacrilege. At the opposite end of the same room, a similar fabric has been chosen for curtains.

glorious arch unimpaired. A shade mounted on the sill and extended upward would discreetly achieve the same result.

With bay and bow windows, there are two main options: hang the window treatment either along the window shape or outside the recess. If privacy is not an issue, the latter is by far the easiest, less light-stealing solution, although you will be effectively sacrificing any usable floor area, or sill display space in the case of bow windows, when the curtains are closed.

Where you want to follow the shape of the window, the available options will be dictated by the window itself. Both a bow-shaped window and a three-sided bay can have a flexible curtain track or a single pole, though the latter will have to be specially made. Alternatively, they can be treated as a series of smaller windows and given individual shades or curtains—lightly gathered to minimize loss of light—hung from separate poles or tracks. What can work well is to combine both approaches, with sheers or shades against the windows, and full-length, possibly false curtains hung outside the window recess, perhaps with a swag across the top to create a theatrical frame.

**opposite** These three solutions to the challenges of dressing a bay window are equally successful. A quirky custom-made wrought-iron rod provides an interesting focal point, while café curtains or more formal London shades suspended within the individual frames obviate the need for specially made poles and show off the windows' architecture to the full.

**above** The horizontal struts in these six shades dramatically enhance the geometrical feel of this window.

**left** By recognizing that the shades in this sunroom need to do very different jobs—screening the view on one side and filtering the sun on the other—a solution was found for these awkwardly shaped windows.

Working with Proportions  51

# London shade

The arrangement of this shade has been designed to allow the security gates on the window to be opened and closed easily, without hindering the look of the window treatment. Its dramatic billowing curves are mounted outside the window recess at ceiling height from a wooden board angled at the corners to emphasize the fullness that comes from the deep inverted pleat on each side of the heading.

## MATERIALS AND EQUIPMENT

plain fabric with a textured weave

matching sewing thread

large carpenter's square and yardstick

touch-and-close tape

½ in (1.5 cm) plastic shade rings

nylon shade cord

shade pull

basic sewing kit

*for the board:*

1¼ in x 4 in (3 x 10 cm) wooden board, the width
of window frame plus 12 in (30 cm) overlap

pencil

saw, drill, plugs, and screws

sandpaper

paint to match fabric

staple gun

2 angle brackets

cleat and screws

3 screw eyes

## MAKING THE BOARD

Mark two points on one long edge of the plank 6 in (15 cm) in from the corners.
Draw a line from each point to the corner below it, then saw along these two lines.
Sand any rough edges and paint the wood to match the fabric. When the paint has
dried, cut a length of touch-and-close tape to fit along the front edge of the board.
Separate the two pieces and staple the hooked side in place. Screw an angle
bracket 12 in (30 cm) from each corner and mount it on the wall, centrally above the
window. Put a screw-eye toward the back of the underside 6 in (15 cm) in from each
corner, and the third 2 in (5 cm)
from the right edge.

## MEASURING

A = length of pelmet board plus
2 in (6 cm)

B = from ceiling to 1¼ in (3 cm)
below bottom edge of frame or sill

## CUTTING OUT

width = A plus 24 in (60 cm) for pleats plus
2 in (4 cm) for hems

depth = B plus 2 in (4 cm) for hems

Cut 2 cords to the following lengths:
2B; 2B plus A

**1** Press a ½-in (1-cm) allowance along each side of the fabric. Fold over a second time to make a double hem and press. Pin, baste, and machine stitch close to the inner fold. Hem the bottom the same way.

**2** Mark the two pleats by cutting three small notches along the top, 7 in (18 cm), 13 in (33 cm), and 19 in (48 cm) in from each corner.

**3** On the wrong side of the fabric, draw a chalk line parallel to each side, in line with the center notch of each pleat. Mark the positions for the rings at 16 in (40 cm) intervals along each line, starting at the bottom edge.

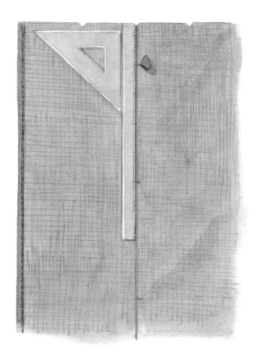

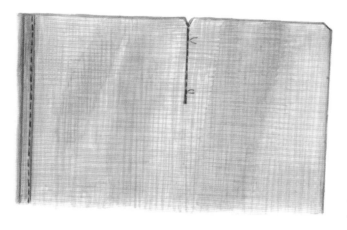

**4** With right sides together, fold the shade lengthwise so the first and third notches at one corner meet. Draw a 4-in (10-cm) chalk line on the wrong side at this point and pin along it. Do the same at the other corner and check the position of the pleats against the board. They should lie across the angles; adjust if necessary. Baste and machine stitch the pleats in place, working extra stitches at each end to secure the row.

**5** Match the center notches to the seams and open out the fabric at each side to make inverted pleats. Pin and baste together through all the layers. Machine stitch ½ in (1 cm) from the edge and press.

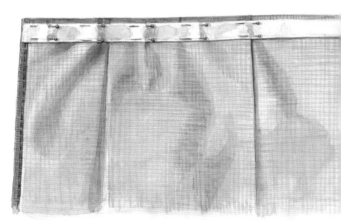

**6** Press under a 1-in (2-cm) allowance along the top of the shade. Pin and baste the second length of touch-and-close tape to the back, ¼ in (5 mm) from the fold. Machine stitch, starting each row from the same end of the tape to prevent the fabric from puckering.

**7** Sew a ring to each of the points marked in step 3.

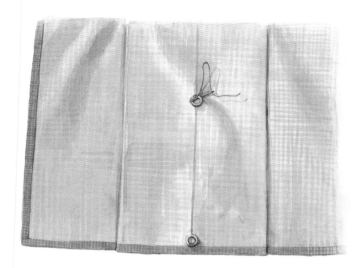

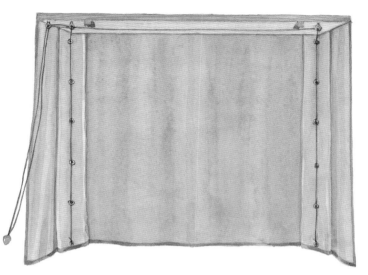

**8** Knot the two cords to the bottom rings and thread them upward. Attach the shade to the strip of wood, lining up the touch-and-close tape carefully. Stand between the shade and the window to complete the stringing. Thread cord on your left (as seen above) through the screw-eye immediately above and then through the eye to the left. Take the other cord through the screw-eye above it, then across through the other two eyes.

**9** Attach the cleat to the right side of the window frame. Trim the cords so they end just below the cleat. Attach the shade pull and knot in place.

**VARIATION**

This simplified version (right and far right) is suitable when the shade does not need to be built around a recess. It is made from two narrow panels of sheer fabric joined with a French seam (see Practicalities, page 136). It is mounted with touch-and-close tape to a narrow strip of wood set within the frame so it lies flat against the window. The rings are attached to the back of the side hems and center seam at 10-in (25-cm) intervals to create two soft curves when the shade is up.

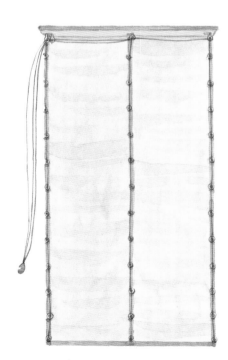

# French doors
## and cupboards

Most French doors and external glazed doors, whether they lead to a terrace, balcony, or backyard, are designed to frame an outside view that should be enjoyed to the full. For this reason, choose a window treatment and a fabric that combine to enhance rather than detract from the vista and let it be appreciated at all times. Plain or subtly patterned fabrics are the obvious contenders. Since the windows will frequently be open, it is a good idea to select fabrics and treatments that are easily laundered because they may soon become grubby with dust and the human traffic passing through.

Unlike most other window styles, French and glazed doors have the practical requirement that access through them should not be restricted, so stationary headings should be avoided. Likewise, heavily gathered or lined

**opposite** A series of disparate glazed doors and windows are unified with the use of eye-catching swagged valances in a bold striped fabric.

**left** Ceiling-mounted rods that keep the curtain away from the window frame are useful for floor-to-ceiling French doors.

**right** Firmly tied back, decorative sheer curtains allow easy access through these French doors while softening the dominating expanse of glass.

**below** At first glance, you wouldn't know these understated curtains were there, so well do they blend into the background.

and interlined curtains are not ideal, especially where there is not enough space for the fabric to hang clear of the doors when the curtains are pulled back. Tiebacks or holdbacks are useful accessories here, both to keep curtains clear of the opening and to prevent them from flapping in the breeze. And even if ease of access is not an overwhelming consideration, because the windows are reasonably wide, for example, bear in mind that any doors that open inward will inevitably catch on full curtains and eventually damage them in the process.

Where the doors will be used only in the summer with any regularity, and the delights of the view are similarly seasonal, consider changing the window treatment in winter, when a heavier, cozier style might be welcome, especially if the doors are at all drafty.

Many of the disadvantages of wide or tall windows apply to French doors, so adapt the relevant solutions to suit the practicalities of a thoroughfare. For example, where there is more than one pair of French doors in a row, breaking up the expanse of glass with a series of individual curtains would probably be impractical, unless they are lightweight enough to be opened well clear of the doors in daytime. Several shades, on the other hand, might work well.

For tall or narrow windows and doors, techniques such as extending the pole or track beyond the window frame to add the appearance of width will have practical as well as visual benefits.

Where you are thinking of mounting shades or curtains directly on the frame of a glazed door, remember that if the door opens out, they will be exposed to the weather.

**above** Extending the curtain pole well beyond the sides of these arched French doors allows the unusually full, boldly checked curtains, with a gypsy-style gathered hem, to hang clear of the doorway during the day. The patterned valance draws the eye up, diverting attention from what has become a wide-looking window.

**right** Where the counters do not allow the curtains to be opened clear of the doorway, lightly gathered panels in a small, obtrusive check are the order of the day. Simple tie tabs suit the informality of setting and can be easily taken down for cleaning.

MATERIALS AND EQUIPMENT
light- to medium-weight fabric
matching sewing thread
heading buckram 4 in (10 cm) deep
curtain hooks
basic sewing kit

**MEASURING**
A = ½ length of pole
B = from bottom of rings to floor

**CALCULATING THE PLEAT ALLOWANCE**
The pleats are 5 in (12 cm) apart with a 2½ in
(6 cm) space at each corner. Divide A by 5 in
(12 cm) to find out how many you will need, and
round up or down to the nearest whole number.
Multiply this figure by 6 in (15 cm) to find out how
much extra fabric is needed to make the pleats.

**CUTTING OUT**
If necessary, join lengths of fabric to the required
width using a narrow French seam (see
Practicalities, page 136).

width = A plus pleat allowance plus 5 in (12 cm) for
hems plus overlap allowance, if required
length = B plus 4½ in (11 cm) for heading allowance
plus 6 in (15 cm) for hems

Cut a length of buckram 1 in (2 cm) shorter than
the width of the curtain panel

# unlined triple-pleat curtains

Unlined curtains are usually made from a lighter weight of fabric than lined
curtains to allow daylight to filter through. Ready-made tapes designed to create
instant pleated headings are easy to use, but it is worth making headings by hand
in the traditional way because they give a crisper, more professional finish and
can be adapted to create accurate pleats on striped or checked fabrics. Buckram
—a coarse cloth stiffened with size—gives rigidity to the headings.

**1** For each curtain, turn under and press a 1¼-in (3-cm) double hem along each side edge and a 3-in (7.5-cm) double hem along the bottom edge.

**2** Mark three points with pins: the corner, the inside edge of the side turning where it meets the hem, and the corresponding point on the hem.

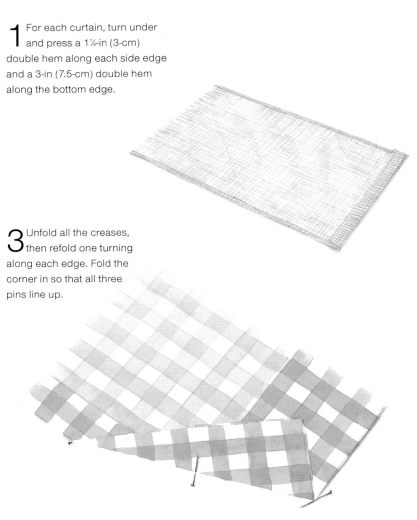

**3** Unfold all the creases, then refold one turning along each edge. Fold the corner in so that all three pins line up.

**4** Press lightly, then refold and pin down the second turnings. Slipstitch the two sides of the miter together, from the corner in.

**5** Pin and baste the side and bottom hems. Machine stitch or slipstitch the side hems, and slipstitch or herringbone stitch the bottom hem.

**6** Press under a ½-in (1-cm) allowance along the top raw edge. Starting ½ in (1 cm) in from one corner, pin the top edge of the buckram under the fold. Baste and machine stitch it in place.

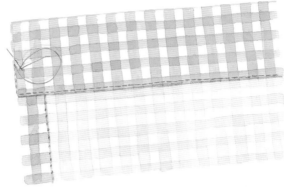

**7** Fold the buckram to the wrong side and press along the fold. Slipstitch the side edges of the fold together.

**8** Using tailor's chalk, mark the positions of the pleats and the gaps between them along the wrong side of the top edge.

**9** Pin two pleat lines together to make a large pleat. Baste and machine stitch on the right side to just below the bottom edge of the buckram.

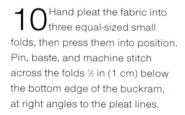

**10** Hand pleat the fabric into three equal-sized small folds, then press them into position. Pin, baste, and machine stitch across the folds ½ in (1 cm) below the bottom edge of the buckram, at right angles to the pleat lines.

**11** Sew a curtain hook securely to the top of each pleat, on the wrong side of the heading. If the curtain is to hang from decorative rings on a pole, the top of the hooks should be ½ in (1 cm) below the top edge of the curtain. If the curtain is to hang from a track, the top of the hooks should be 2 in (5 cm) down, so the track is concealed when the curtains are closed.

**this page** Curtains make inexpensive screens to open shelving in rooms where clutter and mess need disguising. Here, box-pleated panels in an unusual metallic fabric are suspended from a plain metal rod using a heavy-duty combination of eyelets and screw clips. The wipe-clean material is ideal for its setting in a working kitchen.

**opposite, above** This sumptuous living room has been lined with green velvet across its walls, and the same fabric has been chosen to make up the drapes. Lightly gathered with traditional triple pleats and hung from a plain, narrow rod, the curtains make this doorway effectively "disappear" when they are pulled closed.

In some cases, it might be a more practical solution to attach a roll-up shade—which takes up little space when pulled up—to the retaining frame.

For fully or partially glazed internal doors, where privacy or hiding domestic mess are the main concerns rather than light, heat, or noise insulation, consider Roman, Swedish, or plain shades. For a softer look, use decorative panels—an antique dishtowel or a lacy tray cloth are perfect for this use and have the bonus of being relatively instant options requiring little sewing.

Immovable curtains gathered onto sprung curtain wires or narrow rods at the top and bottom of the window also look neat. Choose a lightweight fabric in a plain or small-patterned geometric fabric, as larger-scale patterns will become lost in the tight gathers. Being attached to the frame at the top and bottom keeps the window treatment firmly anchored to the moving door, but has the disadvantage of making it inflexible, so the window is obscured at all times, which should be borne in mind if light is restricted. The gathered-curtain solution works particularly well for glazed or open cupboard doors, introducing a sweet country style in gingham for a kitchen or a more sophisticated look in a sheer fabric for built-in closets in a bedroom.

If the door is recessed in the eaves or positioned in a corner of the room, you may prefer to use hinged portière rods, which mean the curtain can be swung back to one side against the wall when necessary.

**below far left** An antique cabinet that is missing its original glazing is given a new lease of life with lightly gathered panels of gingham set behind chicken wire.

**below centre left** Minimalist white curtains look suitably modern at these floor-to-ceiling French doors while adding a softening and light-filtering touch to the clean lines of a contemporary kitchen.

**below** The rod for these casement-headed door curtains can be easily unscrewed from the door and disassembled when the curtains need cleaning.

# cupboard curtains

A minimal amount of sewing is needed to create these curtains. Each panel is a simple rectangle, hemmed along each side and gathered at the top and bottom. The gingham curtains are drawn up with elastic and pinned in place, while the more formal folds of the plain curtains are created by using sprung curtain wire. Washable lightweight and sheer cotton furnishing or dressmaking fabrics are most suitable because they hang in fine folds. Small prints, solid colors, or geometric stripes and checks work best; large-scale patterns get lost when gathered.

**MATERIALS AND EQUIPMENT**
cotton fabric
matching sewing thread
basic sewing kit

*for the gingham curtains:*
narrow braid elastic
small safety pin
thumbtacks

*for the plain curtains:*
pencil and awl
4 screw-eyes and 4 cup hooks for each curtain
sprung curtain wire
heavy wire cutters

**MEASURING AND CUTTING OUT**
The finished curtain should overlap the glass or mesh by 1¼ in (3 cm) at each side.

width = 1½–2 x width of door panel (depending on weight of fabric) plus 2½ in (6 cm) overlap plus 1½ in (4 cm) hem allowance

length = depth of panel plus 2½ in (6 cm) overlap plus 2½ in (6 cm) for the headings

**MAKING THE CURTAINS**

**1** Iron the fabric to remove any creases. Press under ½ in (1 cm) along each side edge. Press under another ½ in (1 cm) to make a double hem, then pin, baste, and machine stitch close to the inner fold. If the fabric is not the same on both sides, make the hems on the right side.

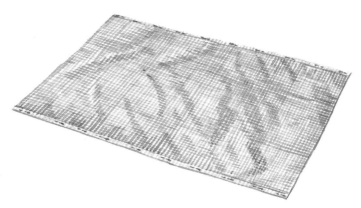

**2** Press under ½ in (1 cm) along the bottom edge, then press under another ¾ in (2 cm). Pin, baste, and machine stitch close to the inner fold to form a narrow channel or casing heading. Do the same at the top edge and finish any loose threads.

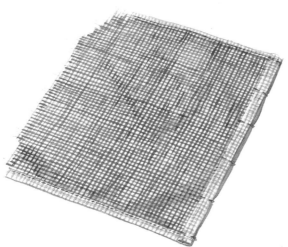

## HANGING THE GINGHAM CURTAINS

1 Cut a length of braid elastic 1½ in (4 cm) shorter than the width of the door panel. Attach a safety pin to one end and pass it along the bottom casing. Draw the elastic through until the loose end is in line with the opening, then stab stitch it securely in place, through the front and back of the casing.

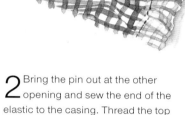

2 Bring the pin out at the other opening and sew the end of the elastic to the casing. Thread the top casing the same way.

3 With hems and casings facing the door, attach the curtain to the inside of the cupboard using thumbtacks at the top and bottom edges.

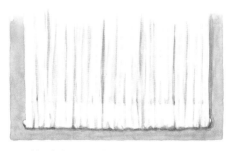

## HANGING THE PLAIN CURTAINS

1 Mark four points on the back of the cupboard door, 1¼ in (3 cm) from each corner of the opening. Use an awl to make a hole at each mark and screw the hooks into the door so they face up.

3 Cut the wire to length and twist the second eye in place. Do the same with the second piece of wire.

4 Feed the two wires into the top and bottom casings; the fabric will gather up as it goes through.

5 Hook the top wire in place so the hems and casings face the door, then slip the bottom screw-eyes over the hooks.

2 Twist a screw-eye into one end of the sprung wire and loop it over a hook. Stretch the wire across to the second hook—it should be taut but not too tight—and make a pencil mark on the wire where they meet.

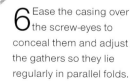

6 Ease the casing over the screw-eyes to conceal them and adjust the gathers so they lie regularly in parallel folds.

**this page** Simple linen drapes in a soothing shade of blue wrap up a daybed, to create a cozy, private retreat in an open-plan apartment.

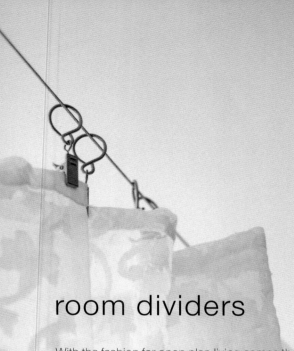

main picture Lightweight fabrics, such as this cotton voile, can be suspended from a tension wire to create an unobtrusive divider.

above right A modern take on the beaded curtain: lengths of chrome chain make an unusual screen.

center right Unusual fabrics, like this dévoré velvet sheer, can elevate a functional screen to a thing of beauty.

below right In a small studio where a room-width divider would restrict space, a mosquito net is a clever way to camouflage the bed from the living room during the day.

# room dividers

With the fashion for open-plan living comes the predicament of what to do about privacy and the inevitable mess on view for all the world to see, not to mention the echoes and drafts that big spaces encourage. Screens and dividers neatly provide a solution by allowing personal spaces and the detritus of everyday life to be hidden out of sight when necessary, while still allowing that all-important feeling of space and freedom of movement to remain.

Specialized manufacturers have been quick to come up with attractive solutions. Stiffened or weighted panels that glide along barely seen channels set in the ceiling, stacking up like a deck of cards when not in use, are now available. Pulley systems operated by a cord or an electric motor prevent the leading edges from becoming grubby through handling. These panels suit the minimalist, modern character of today's pared-down interiors and can be layered to create different effects and degrees of translucency. And, if they are attached to the gliding system with touch-and-close tape, they can be changed with the seasons.

Variations on this theme might include Venetian, vertical, or roll-up shades. But if panels or shades are too austere for your tastes, or for the rest of the room scheme, it is equally feasible to use any style of reversible curtain—remember the dividers will be seen from both sides. In fact, the modern, relaxed styles of heading, such as loops or ties, are perfect since they have no "wrong" side.

# SHEERS

Sheers were once, at best, the lacy first line of defense against the destructive forces of sunlight and smog lurking at every Victorian householder's (heavily dressed) windows. At worst, they were the twitching, graying nylon screen behind which nosy neighbors hid.

Now, happily, sheers stand alone as desirable window treatments in their own right, with a vast selection of natural fibers to choose from. In the form of curtains, especially, sheers are essentially feminine, floaty confections that add softness to a room scheme. To play down their girlie connotations, team them with masculine poles and tiebacks, reduce the amount of fabric used, or consider colored sheers in muted, earthy tones.

**this page** Sheer fabrics with embroidered motifs are available, but you can add your own trimmings with ribbons and fringing.

**opposite, above left** Tiny bows of colored ribbon have been hand-stitched to this plain cotton curtain.

**opposite, above right** Two-styles-in-one: the hem of the sheer on the left has been dip-dyed to create an irregular border of color, while the sheer on the right is a self-patterned voile that has been machine-dyed solid yellow.

**opposite, below left** This embroidered sari has been dyed pink to fill a girlie bedroom with a rosy glow.

**opposite, below right** Delicate machine-embroidered dragonflies are scattered across this sun-filled space.

Although sheer curtains are the ideal solution when privacy or disguising an unattractive view are the main issues, rather than light, heat, or noise insulation, bear in mind that where they are to remain closed, the more gathered the material, the less light will penetrate into the room. Lightly gathered curtains, minimal flat panels, or carefully made shades (remember, every seam will be highlighted against the window) are a useful compromise where the window architecture deserves to be on show but the view doesn't. However, they do have the disadvantage that at night, with a light on, they will quite revealingly live up to their name, so secondary curtains or a plain shade mounted close to the window frame might be an additional requirement.

For a lightweight sheer fabric to work as a shade or flat panel, it will need to be stiffened or weighted down. Many shade makers will treat client-supplied fabrics with special chemicals to stiffen the material before assembling.

**far left** Fabrics don't necessarily have to be labeled "sheers" to do the job. This lightweight gingham, made into a simple Swedish shade, is rendered semitranslucent and makes the most of available light through this small but sunny window.

**left** Clouds of embroidered voile positively glow in this garden room. Lightweight materials are best suited to simple headings like the tape ties used here with an inexpensive bamboo stake.

**above** An antique lace wedding veil has been charmingly reinvented as a curtain screen, with a quirky "valance" provided by a bundle of twigs secured with twine. Note how the sheer fabric allows the leaded windows to be appreciated.

# appliquéd half-panel

Only the minimum of screening is needed for privacy at this nineteenth-century window. A simple geometrically patterned panel decorated with hand-appliquéd motifs accentuates the cobalt glass border and the elegant shape of the frame. This technique is usually associated with folk-art quilts and patchwork, but used sparingly, as here, it can have a much more contemporary feel.

**MATERIALS AND EQUIPMENT**
pencil and tracing paper
thin cardboard
white cotton sheeting or dressmaking fabric
checked fabric panel (such as gingham)
matching sewing thread
basic sewing kit

1 Enlarge the flower and leaf templates (right) as necessary. Trace the solid outlines, transfer them to thin cardboard, and cut out.

2 Using a dressmaker's pen, draw around the cardboard onto the cotton fabric. Draw a second line ¼ in (5 mm) in, following the broken line on the template. This represents the seam allowance. Add the center veins to the leaf and cut out the shape.

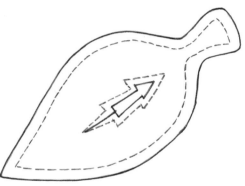

3 Clip the curved edges at intervals of approximately ⅜ in (8 mm) so they lie flat. Cut small notches into the outside curves and clip the inside curves to just outside the pen line. Cut out the center of the leaf as indicated.

4 Carefully turn under the seam allowance as far as the line, pressing it in place between finger and thumb. Baste it down using small stitches. Fold over the surplus fabric at the point and stem of the leaf.

5 Pin and baste the flowers and leaves in position on the panel, so one motif will hang in front of each pane. Sew down by hand using neat slipstitches. Press lightly using a pressing cloth and hang at the window.

Alternatively, there are various do-it-yourself kits relying on aerosol sprays that can be used at home. Solutions that could add weight and definition to flimsy fabrics include a contrasting edging made from a heavier fabric stitched along the hem or around all four sides to make a frame; one or more narrow poles hidden in horizontal casings; a border of heavy trimming along the lower edges; appliqué-style decoration; or even old-fashioned curtain weights sewn into the hem. Whichever method you use, remember that these are very lightweight fabrics, so don't go overboard; otherwise, the fabric will end up distorted.

For all sheer curtains, but for white or off-white fabrics especially, washability should be an important consideration because they will soon pick up dust and begin to look dingy (hence infamous the gray nylons of old). For this reason, if the fabric is not preshrunk, machine wash it on the correct cycle before making your curtains, or make allowance for future shrinkage when you calculate the measurements. It will also be helpful to choose a heading or style of shade that can easily be undone to allow for regular laundering—softly pleated shades or curtains with tie-top headings, for instance.

**opposite** Dressmaking fabric
includes some inspirational sheers
like this prettily dotted net which,
away from its intended setting,
manages to not look overtly bridal.
Using a transparent fabric over a
background wall color will alter the
end result. Generally, pastel colors
work best with white sheers, though
this apricot creates an interesting
effect. Allowing the curtain to
"puddle" on the floor enhances the
feminine look.

**this page** The design of this delicate
silk paisley is shown off to great
effect when it is lit from behind. A
beaded trim along the leading edge
adds definition and structure.

# bordered sheer panel

A minimal look works well in a period interior. The clean lines of this bordered panel complement the architectural detail of the Victorian townhouse window and are a welcome modern alternative to a gathered net. The striped frame is mitered at the corners and made in two layers so the panel can be reversed.

**MATERIALS AND EQUIPMENT**
sheer fabric
striped upholstery fabric
matching sewing thread
ruler
curtain clips
basic sewing kit

**MEASURING**
A = width of frame
B = from bottom of pole to 2 in (5 cm) below bottom edge of window

**CUTTING OUT**
Match the stripes exactly on the border strips, so they meet at the corners.

*main panel:*
width = A minus 6 in (15 cm) for border
length = B minus 6 in (15 cm) for border
Mark a point ½ in (1.5 cm) in from each corner.

*long borders (cut 4):*
width = 4 in (11 cm)
length = A plus 1 in (3 cm) for seams

*short borders (cut 4):*
width = 4 in (11 cm)
length = B plus 1 in (3 cm) for seams

**1** The ends of the borders are trimmed at 45 degrees. Working on the wrong side, mark a point along what will be the inside edge of the first short border, 4 in (11 cm) in from the left corner. Using a dressmaker's pen, draw a line up to the other corner and cut along it. Shape the other corners, making sure that all the inside edges are the same color.

**2** Lightly press and unfold a ½-in (1.5-cm) seam allowance along both short edges and the longest edge of each border panel.

**3** With right sides together, pin and baste the inside edge of a short border to the top of the panel. Line the creases up with the dots at the corners. Turn over, then pin and baste a second short border to the other side, so the right side faces down.

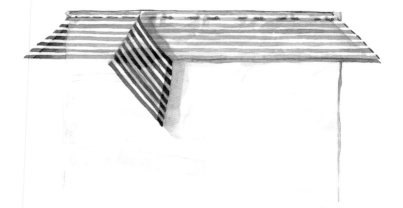

**4** Machine stitch through all three layers, ½ in (1.5 cm) from the edge. Refold the seam allowance at the ends of the two borders and press the strips away from the panel.

**5** Attach the other two short and the four long border strips in the same way. Clip off the surplus fabric at each corner ¼ in (5 mm) from the corner.

**6** Refold the seam allowance along the outside edges of the border strips. Pin and baste the seam allowance under all the way around the border.

**7** Join the mitered corners on both sides of the panel with slipstitch, sewing from the outer edge of the corner in.

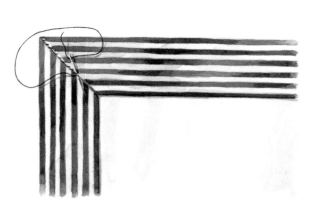

**8** Baste the two borders together around the outside, tucking in any surplus fabric at the corners. Machine stitch ⅛ in (3 mm) from the edge. Press the panel and attach to the curtain rod with metal clips.

# DETAILS

Just as the right accessories will transform an understated little black dress into a showstopper, so well-chosen poles, finials, tiebacks, trimmings, and headings can transform simple or inexpensive window treatments into individual, characterful, and eye-catching features. But use these details with restraint —remember, there's nothing worse than looking overdressed!

Sometimes these "accessories" are pure serendipity: lucky hand-me-downs and antique-store finds; sometimes they come from an afternoon's research in a specialized store—don't limit yourself to retailers dedicated to interiors, though; look in dressmaking departments, too, where potential crossovers include sequins, sari ribbons, and lace edgings. Alternatively, pure invention comes into play, transforming found objects like driftwood, seashells, sea glass, and "witches' stones" (the beach pebbles with holes through the middle) into curtain "jewelry."

Remember that the plainer the curtain fabric and style, the more the tieback, trim, or finial will clamor for attention. Conversely, the more decorative the curtain, the less these details will be noticed.

**opposite, above left** Simple white drapes with a stationary heading over an arched doorway are elevated from the ordinary with the addition of handmade cutout leaf covers to hide the tiebacks and heading hooks.

**opposite, above right** An ornate carved and gilded finial steals the show partnered with a plain wooden pole and understated plaid cotton curtains.

**opposite, below left** An opulent pewter tassel can transcend period styling in a resolutely contemporary interior.

**opposite, below right** Coordinated bobble fringe adds texture while maintaining the naturalistic style of these muslin curtains.

**this page** Casual observers might miss these charming fossil knobs, the only decoration on a rough silk panel, but once spotted, they lend character to the otherwise minimalist styling.

**opposite** The traditional styles of heading, like these neat triple pleats, really show their pedigree when the curtains are opened and closed, gliding, as they do, with the folds of fabric falling into regimented order.

**this page** These room dividers make the point that screening does not have to be floor-to-ceiling to be effective. An inventive arrangement of bent copper rods attached through metal eyelets in the fabric both suspends the frayed panels of linen from the ceiling and weights them at floor level. The result offers both privacy and demarcation while allowing light from the windows to spill from one area of the open-plan space to another.

# headings

Today, the trend for simple and lightly gathered curtains has, in many situations, overshadowed the role of more complicated, ornate headings like hand-stitched goblet pleats, lattice pleats and box pleats. However, these formal styles should not be dismissed as "old-fashioned" or "too fussy." They still have the ability to add that special "something" that is both the perfect foil to the most expensive fabrics and a way of adding glamour to the cheapest. And as many of the traditional headings can now be replicated with specialized ready-made heading tapes, there is no excuse not to go the extra length, should the situation demand it.

Of the straightforward heading tapes, the most versatile options are narrow gathering tape, which replicates a drawstring effect and is only suitable for small or lightweight curtains such as sheers; pencil-pleat tape, which creates an even row of small parallel pleats, for use on medium- to heavyweight fabrics; and deep-pleat tape, which is similar to pencil-pleat tape but has more cords to create a fuller, more stylized heading. A trick worth considering when using narrow gathering tape is to sew it 4 inches (10 cm) or more below the top of the curtain (remember to include this additional amount when calculating the overall length), which results in an attractively casual, floppy top edge.

Another traditional but relatively unfussy treatment is the café-style casing that can be used for full- or half-length curtains. For this style, a channel is stitched along the top of the curtain panel through which the pole or curtain wire is threaded. The gathered heading is then effectively set, with the curtains held back when necessary with a tieback or holdback. Again, this casing can be positioned below the top of the curtain to create a soft edging along the top edge.

Beyond the traditional styles, the more contemporary innovations combine the function of heading, hook, and curtain ring in one. Simple tabs constructed from the curtain fabric are either looped over the pole or held in place with buttons or touch-and-close tape. This style works well with panels that hang flat or in loose gathers when closed. Similar, but more pretty and feminine, are tie-on headings, which can be practically any width, from narrow and neat to broad and flouncy.

For instant, no-sew curtains, curtain clips in all their variations are heaven-sent. Available in a choice of metallic finishes and strengths, they can transform simple hemmed panels, antique quilts, plaid blankets, lacy tablecloths, and saris—in fact, any approximately rectangular piece of fabric—into an instant curtain. If the panel is too long, merely fold the top over to create an integral valance.

More high-tech in appearance are metal eyelets, which come in several diameters, the narrowest of which could be hung over hooks on the wall for a semi-stationary panel or strung from tension wire, while the largest are big enough to thread straight onto a narrow curtain pole.

An advantage of these contemporary heading styles is that they don't have a wrong side. This means that should you want to use a double-sided fabric or a lined panel—which has the bonus of improving the view of the window when seen from the outside—you can make changes to your decorative scheme with the seasons or your moods simply by reversing the way it is hung.

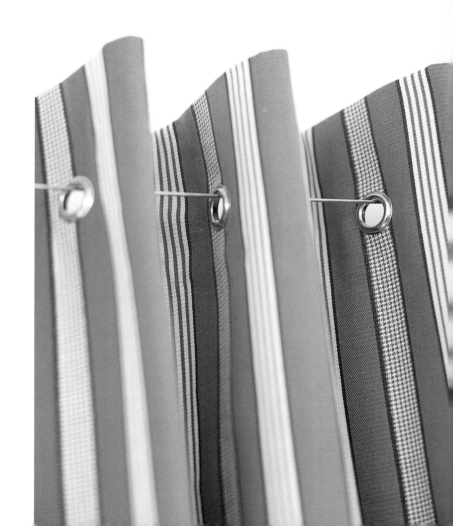

**near right** Loosely gathered pencil pleats married to a smart damask look formal but not too traditional.

**center right** For an unobtrusive heading, run a double hem along the top and add ties made from the same fabric as the curtains.

**far right** Traditional hand-sewn pleats take on a contemporary look in unbleached linen.

**left** Metal eyelets suspended from a tension wire create a nautical look with a blue and white striped fabric.

**above** Is it a curtain or is it a shade? Edging muslin with jute tape provides a sturdy frame for a stationary panel—a simple variation on a Roman shade.

**right** Positioning plain gathering tape well below the top of the curtain creates a casual, floppy effect and helps disguise an unattractive track or pole.

# jasmine-headed curtain

This charming, quirky curtain, described by its maker as a "quick fix," requires the bare minimum of sewing. It was created by simply folding a double length of fabric in half and attaching twig circlets—available from craft suppliers or florists—to the top edge in place of curtain rings. Lengths of realistic silk jasmine flowers wind through the rings and act as a tieback to complete the natural theme. The effect is theatrical and ideally suited to a doorway such as this, which is in constant use, so the curtain is pulled back at all times.

MATERIALS AND EQUIPMENT

heavy cotton fabric
matching sewing thread
silk embroidery thread
large crewel needle
twig circlets
silk jasmine flowers
tieback hook
drill, screws, and plugs
basic sewing kit

MEASURING

A = width of doors or window plus 16 in (40 cm)
B = from bottom of rings to floor

CUTTING OUT

Using a flat seam, join lengths of fabric to the required width. Make sure the selvages lie on the outside edges to avoid having to make side hems.

width = 1½ x A
length = 3 x B

**1** Run a ¾-in (2-cm) double hem along the top and bottom edges.

**2** Lay the fabric on the floor and fold in half lengthwise with wrong sides together. This will be easier if you have somebody to help you maneuver the fabric.

**3** Using a dressmaker's pen and starting at the leading-edge corner, mark the positions for the rings along the top. They should be at intervals of about 8 in (20 cm).

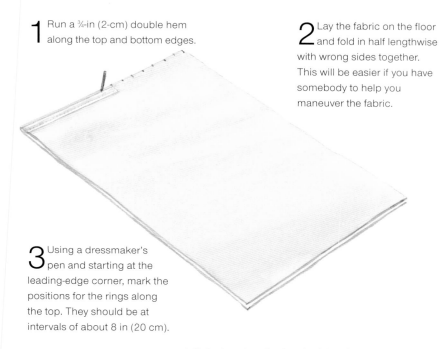

**4** Cut a long length of embroidery floss and thread all six strands through a large crewel needle. Leaving the end loose, sew the first circlet in place by passing the needle through the top edge of the curtain and between the outer twigs three times.

**5** Knot the two ends securely. Wrap the loose thread firmly around the loop, then tie off and trim the ends, leaving two short "tails." Attach the rest of the circlets the same way, then hang the curtain.

**6** Weave lengths of silk flowers through the circlets to form loops. Let the ends trail down over the curtain.

**7** Screw the tieback hook to the adjacent wall about halfway down the door. Tie the curtain back with the remaining lengths of jasmine and secure them over the hook.

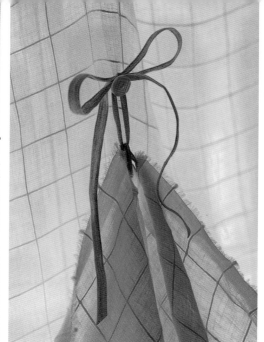

# tiebacks and holdbacks

Although tiebacks have been on the receiving end of some bad press of late for their somewhat prissy lineage, they have practical as well as decorative advantages, even in today's laidback rooms. They are a must, for instance, at French doors, where drapes would inevitably flap in the breeze without them. They are also necessary for stationary or false curtains, where the objective is to make the window treatment look as full and realistic as possible. In fact, any curtain that needs to be restrained if the window or opening is not to be obscured—including door curtains, heavily gathered drapes designed to hang in decorative folds, and bed curtains—all need to be held back in some way for some, if not all, of the time.

The most attractive of the traditional styles for holdbacks are plain or decorative metal cloak pins and u-shaped brackets. Cloak pins are metal or wooden disks mounted on a short rod secured to the wall or window frame. The old-fashioned bracket-style holdbacks actually work particularly well with the present vogue for metal poles and rings.

Other traditional styles that can provide inspiration include large tassels hung from cord, which can look very grand in silk but quite relaxed in humbler materials such as cotton or jute.

**opposite, main and far left** A functional black-painted metal hook is the perfect foil for the informally draped linen sheet at the window of this sun-drenched room. A second sheet has been cleverly nailed in position on the beams to act as a valance, equally in keeping with the relaxed atmosphere of the setting.

**opposite, center left** This printed sheer curtain has been gathered up in soft folds and "gift wrapped" with an rosette of dark translucent ribbon.

**opposite, center right** The bottom corner of this sheer linen panel can be held up during the day by looping the simple tape bow over an antique button that has been sewn on just below the heading.

**opposite, right** A piece of plaid ribbon has been stitched to the center of a wider length of pink taffeta ribbon and tied around a gauzy floor-length curtain to make an informal tieback, reminiscent of a Scottish country dancer's sash.

**right** Sometimes the traditional favorites are still the best choice: this silky rope tieback with its coordinating bullion tassel adds a classic touch to a pink velvet curtain.

**below right** This sculptural brass holdback, set at sill height, is an elegant and unobtrusive way of keeping the folds of a heavy linen curtain in place. This treatment would work equally well in a period or modern interior.

Crescent-shaped, reinforced fabric tiebacks and fabric plaits, bows, and rosettes are now arguably in the same camp as balloon shades: irredeemable and best avoided!

Otherwise, be inventive and choose a tieback which will complement your curtain. Something as simple as a piece of rope with a loop at each end to slip over a wall hook or a loose length of ribbon would do the job stylishly without looking too contrived. Or what about a silk scarf, salvaged doorknob, leather belt, or chunky vintage necklace (pearls look stunning with a sheer fabric, while wooden beads make a sweet partner to a cheery gingham)?

It is a good idea to set your tiebacks in place after the curtains have been hung at the window, having first experimented with different positions. They should be arranged directly below the end of the track or pole, and as a rule they should be roughly two-thirds of the way down floor-to-ceiling drapes, so the fabric will be pulled back in an elegant curve when the curtains are open. If the tiebacks are placed higher up, more of the window will be revealed and the room will be lighter, but the proportions are not always so pleasing. If they are lower, the curtains will hang in fuller, more theatrical folds.

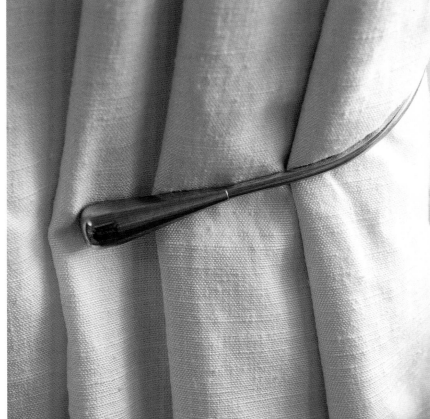

# padded holdback

The deep folds of this silk curtain are restrained with a padded cloak-pin, giving an extravagant, sculpted appearance. The woodwork can be avoided by simply covering a ready-made holdback.

**MATERIALS AND EQUIPMENT**

4 in (10 cm) disk of ⅘-in (2-cm) thick board
4 in (10 cm) length of ⅘ in (2 cm) doweling
sandpaper
drill
fabric
PVA adhesive
2 in (5 cm) screw
thick synthetic batting
button thread
double-ended screw (available from specialized hardware stores)
plug (if necessary)
screwdriver
basic sewing kit

**CUTTING OUT**

*fabric:*
5 in (12 cm) square
10 in (25 cm) circle

*batting:*
3 in (7.5 cm) circle
4 in (10 cm) circle
6 in (15 cm) circle

**1** Sand the disk and doweling to remove any sharp edges. Drill a hole through the center of the disk and into both ends of the doweling.

**2** Press a ½-in (1-cm) hem along one edge of the fabric square and stick down with adhesive. Coat the wrong side with adhesive and leave until almost dry. Wrap the fabric around the doweling with the hem on the outside edge and a ½-in (1-cm) overlap at each end. Trim the overlap to ¼ in (5 mm).

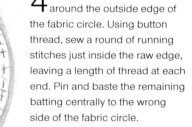

**3** Screw the disk to one end of the doweling. Glue the medium-sized circle of batting to the disk, then glue the smallest circle on top of it.

**4** Baste a ½-in (1-cm) allowance around the outside edge of the fabric circle. Using button thread, sew a round of running stitches just inside the raw edge, leaving a length of thread at each end. Pin and baste the remaining batting centrally to the wrong side of the fabric circle.

**6** Secure the double-ended screw to the end of the doweling. Attach the holdback to the window frame or wall, using a plug if it is to be set into plaster.

**5** Place the fabric over the disk and pull up the gathers around the doweling. Ease the allowance to the wrong side, then knot the ends of the thread and sew them through the fabric to secure the gathers.

**this page** Binding the top and bottom of the integral valance on these sheers with narrow scarlet ribbon both highlights its presence and draws attention to the meringuelike fullness of the curtains.

**opposite, above left** This luxurious tasseled fringe is shown to great effect against a subtle cream-on-cream crewelwork fabric.

**opposite, above center** A labor of love, this intricate scalloped leading edge would take hours to make, but creates a dramatic feature, especially against the pale curtain fabric.

**opposite, above right** A military-style stripe is achieved by using two different widths of braid sewn on top of one another.

**opposite, below** A trimming should be heavy enough in comparison with the curtain fabric to bring definition to the shape, but not heavy enough to distort it. Here lightweight bobble fringe works well with flimsy voile.

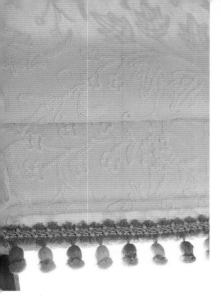

# trims and decorations

In the category of curtain details, the trimmings offer the greatest scope for imagination—and fun. Of the ready-made options, ribbons are the most understated, timeless, and inexpensive (trimmings can easily cost more per yard than the fabric). With their near relatives, patterned braids, ribbons come in all manner of fabrics, including velvet, satin, silk, organza, and wool, and you needn't restrict yourself to those made for furnishings. Endlessly versatile, they can be fashioned into tiebacks, tie-tops, edgings, or to hide a seam where two different fabrics are joined.

Fringe, either cut, tasseled, beaded, bobble, or twisted bullion, comes in every style, from short and discreet to downright shaggy and attention grabbing. It works best used along the leading edge of generously gathered curtains, where not only is the fringe seen to best advantage, silhouetted against the window, but attention can be drawn to the fullness of the curve. Fringes also work well as an embellishment to the bottom of a valance or shade. Indeed, rows of fringe sewn along every section of a Roman shade look amazing when the shade is pleated up—like a 1920s flapper's dress.

Unsurprisingly, the offbeat approach to curtains has infiltrated the realm of trimmings. Quirky ideas include sequins and antique pearl or horn buttons scattered along hems and leading edges. Trims needn't add a luxurious or stylized effect—found objects like shells and feathers sewn along a ribbon can make delicate homemade trims and capture the trend for all things natural.

# zigzag valance

Valances were traditionally used to hide curtain tracks, but this updated version adds visual interest to the top of a plain Roman shade. When the shade is fully up, the pleats are concealed by the zigzag edging. The exact size and shape of the triangles will depend on the width of your window frame: try cutting out a full-sized version in paper to check that the proportions work before you start sewing.

MAKING THE TEMPLATE
Calculate the width of the triangular points by dividing the width of the valance by the number required—a 36-in (90-cm) wide window will require ten 3½-in (9-cm) triangles. Cut an equilateral triangle from thin cardboard, with each side equal to this measurement. If you prefer to have longer, narrower points, simply make your template into an isosceles triangle, with two longer, equal sides. (The simplest way to do this is to draw a baseline of the required width; set a compass to the required depth of the points and mark the apex of the triangle with the compass positioned at each end of the baseline in turn.) Draw a vertical line down the center of the template to divide it in half.

MATERIALS AND EQUIPMENT
pencil
thin cardboard
drawing compass and yardstick
solid fabric
matching sewing thread
⅘-in (2-cm) wide touch-and-close tape
basic sewing kit

*for the board:*
1¼ in x 4 in (3 x 10 cm) wood or 2D, the width of window frame plus 2 in (5 cm) overlap at each side
sandpaper
paint to match fabric
2 angle brackets
screwdriver, drill, plugs, and screws
staple gun

CUTTING OUT
cut front and back alike
width = width of pelmet board plus 9 in (22 cm)
depth = 9 in (22 cm)

1 Sand the board and paint it to match the fabric. When dry, screw the two angle brackets to the underside, 4 in (10 cm) in from each end.

2 Cut a length of touch-and-close tape to fit around the sides and front edge. Separate the two pieces and staple the hooked side around the front and sides of the board. Mount the board in place above the window using plugs.

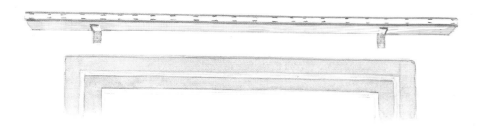

**3** Mark the seam allowance on the wrong side of the back panel: using a dressmaker's pen and a yardstick, draw three lines ½ in (1 cm) in from the sides and the bottom edge.

**4** Starting at the bottom left corner, match the center and base of the template up to the lines. Draw along the right edge of the template, then draw a series of triangles along the bottom line, ending with another half-triangle.

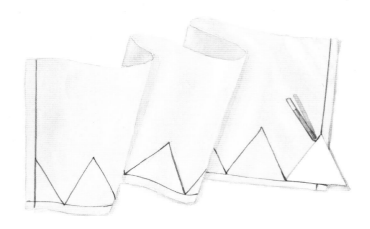

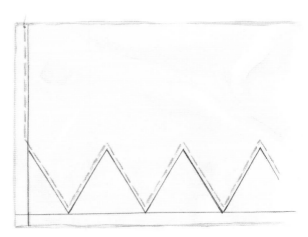

**5** Pin the front and back panels with right sides together, then baste along the sides and close to the zigzag line.

**6** Stitch along the drawn lines, then cut away the excess fabric, snipping in between the triangles and clipping the points so they will lie flat. Turn right side out, easing the points into shape with a knitting needle. Press, then machine stitch all around the seam ⅛ in (3 mm) from the edge.

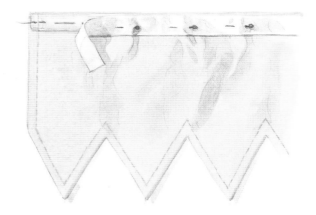

**7** Baste the top edges together, then press under a ½-in (1-cm) allowance. Pin and baste the remaining strip of touch-and-close tape over the raw edges. Machine stitch along the top and bottom edges of the tape. Start both rows of stitching from the same edge to prevent the fabric from puckering.

**8** Mount the valance on the board, carefully matching the two pieces of tape.

# ruched valance

Crisp cotton and natural linen are combined to make this simple valance. It is gathered onto a sprung wire and hung in front of a sheer white curtain. The double heading creates a decorative ruffle, which also conceals a plain utilitarian shade that gives added privacy to the room.

MATERIALS AND EQUIPMENT
white cotton fabric
unbleached linen
matching sewing thread
yardstick
pencil
awl
2 screw-eyes and 2 cup hooks
sprung curtain wire
wire cutters
basic sewing kit

MEASURING AND CUTTING OUT
The measurements are for a valance approximately 16 in (40 cm) deep: adjust them for a taller or shorter window.

*cotton panel:*
width = 2 x width of window
depth = 21 in (53 cm)

*linen border:*
width = 2 x width of window
depth = 7 in (18 cm)

**1** Pin the border to the panel along one long edge with wrong sides together. Baste, then machine stitch ⅜ in (8 mm) from the edge. Trim the seam allowance back to ¼ in (6 mm).

**2** Refold the seam so the raw edges are enclosed and press lightly along the stitch line. Machine stitch ⅜ in (8 mm) from the fold to make a French seam. Press the seam allowance down.

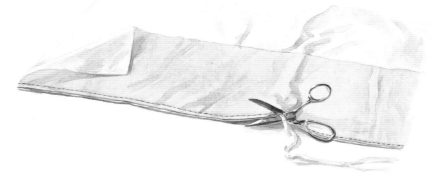

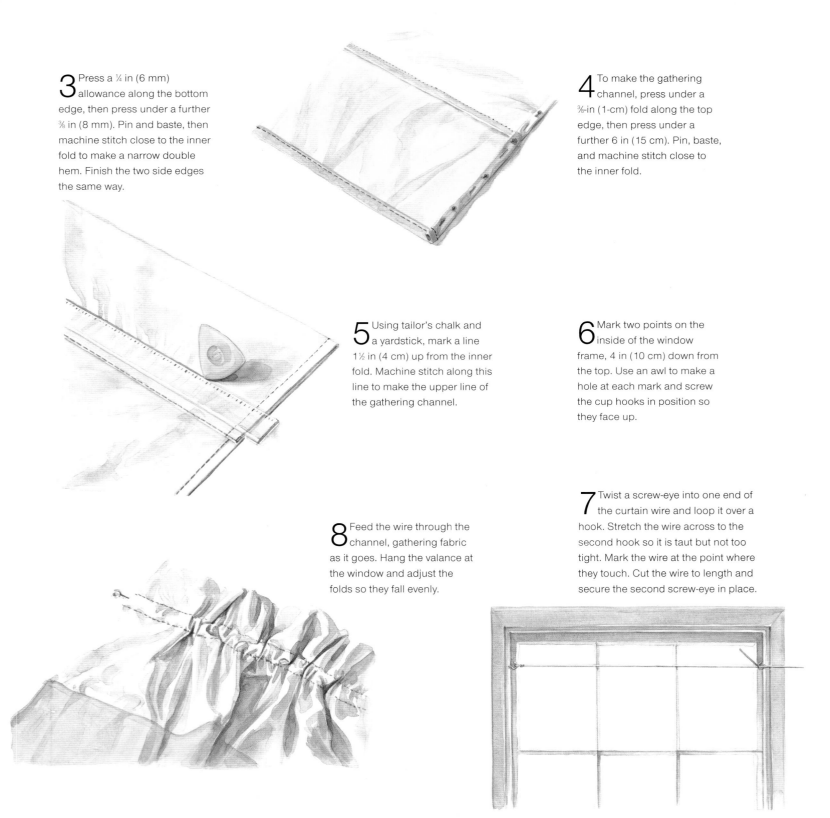

**3** Press a ¼ in (6 mm) allowance along the bottom edge, then press under a further ⅜ in (8 mm). Pin and baste, then machine stitch close to the inner fold to make a narrow double hem. Finish the two side edges the same way.

**4** To make the gathering channel, press under a ⅜-in (1-cm) fold along the top edge, then press under a further 6 in (15 cm). Pin, baste, and machine stitch close to the inner fold.

**5** Using tailor's chalk and a yardstick, mark a line 1½ in (4 cm) up from the inner fold. Machine stitch along this line to make the upper line of the gathering channel.

**6** Mark two points on the inside of the window frame, 4 in (10 cm) down from the top. Use an awl to make a hole at each mark and screw the cup hooks in position so they face up.

**7** Twist a screw-eye into one end of the curtain wire and loop it over a hook. Stretch the wire across to the second hook so it is taut but not too tight. Mark the wire at the point where they touch. Cut the wire to length and secure the second screw-eye in place.

**8** Feed the wire through the channel, gathering fabric as it goes. Hang the valance at the window and adjust the folds so they fall evenly.

# room by room

LIVING SPACES

KITCHENS

BEDROOMS

CHILDREN'S ROOMS

BATHROOMS

**below, right and far right** This row of neutral linen curtains disguises different window styles. Hanging them in front of a narrow fabric-covered valance adds to the tailored effect.

**opposite, center and below** A chic silk stripe is used for this pleated and swagged valance and also edges the translucent silk curtains, creating a frame around the attractive sash window.

# LIVING SPACES

The living space is by definition the place we spend most of our leisure time at home, whether alone, with family or entertaining. It is also likely to have the largest windows: curved or three-sided bays, floor-to-ceiling sashes, and French doors traditionally characterize the most prestigious rooms in a house.

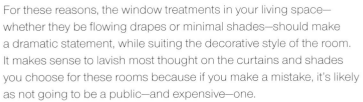

For these reasons, the window treatments in your living space—whether they be flowing drapes or minimal shades—should make a dramatic statement, while suiting the decorative style of the room. It makes sense to lavish most thought on the curtains and shades you choose for these rooms because if you make a mistake, it's likely as not going to be a public—and expensive—one.

In today's informal homes with their open-plan layouts, most living spaces—the double living room in an old row house, for instance—must meet the requirements of both a family room for relaxation and a formal reception room for entertaining. That is to say they need to look formal yet cozy and be stylish yet resilient enough to take the rough and tumble of everyday life.

**this page** Cream damask drapes are a subtle but luxurious foil to the dominating architecture of the verandah seen beyond the window.

**opposite, main picture** Lengths of lilac voile doubled over a pole and dressed with a wool shawl make an instant window treatment in this bohemian apartment.

**opposite, above right** These almost transparent white Swedish shades preserve the striking window architecture and the monochrome decorating scheme of this chic loft apartment.

**opposite, center right** Allowing full-length drapes to fall in soft folds on the floor creates an impractical but luxurious effect, easily justified in a formal room.

**opposite, below right** Panels of solid color can be used vertically as well as horizontally to create interesting effects. Here lighter-colored panels are used to create additional screening during the day in this well-lit room. Positioning the darker panels on the outside of the window creates a framing effect.

# Roman shade

This type of Roman shade is made from a lined rectangular panel, weighted by a lath, with cords on the reverse side. It is hung from a strip of wood, which can be set in a window recess or mounted on a wall. A close-woven cotton fabric such as ticking is easy to sew and will withstand heavy use.

MATERIALS AND EQUIPMENT
white lining fabric
ticking or similar striped fabric
yardstick
½ in (1.5 cm) plastic rings
matching sewing thread
wooden lath, ¾ in (2 cm) shorter than finished width of shade
1¼ x 1¼ in (3 cm x 3 cm) strip of wood, ¼ in (5 mm) shorter than finished width of shade
drill, screwdriver, and plugs
3 small screw-eyes
staple gun
nylon shade cord
small safety pin
shade pull
cleat and screws
basic sewing kit

*if shade is to hang in a window recess:*
4 long screws and plugs

*if shade is to hang outside a window recess or over a frame:*
2 small angle brackets, screws, and plugs
If the shade is to be mounted on the wall, the ends and underside of the wooden strip will be visible, so it should be painted to match the color of the shade.

MEASURING
*if shade is to hang in a window recess:*
A = width of recess minus ¾ in (2 cm)
B = from top of recess to sill

*if shade is to hang outside a window recess or over a frame:*
A = width of frame or recess plus 2½ in (6 cm)
B = from top of strip of wood to 1¼ in (3 cm) below bottom edge of frame

CUTTING OUT
*shade and lining alike:*
width = A plus 1½ in (4 cm)
depth= B plus 5 in (12 cm)

3 cords cut to the following lengths: 2B; 2B plus ¼A; 2B plus A

**1** Using tailor's chalk, mark a line down the center of the right side of the lining, then draw two more lines 2 in (5 cm) in from each long edge. Starting 6 in (15 cm) up from the bottom edge, mark a series of 12-in (30-cm) intervals along each line. Leave a space of at least 8 in (20 cm) at the top to accommodate the shade when it is pulled up.

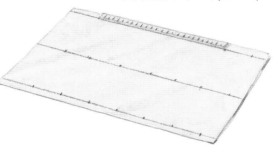

**2** Handstitch a small plastic ring securely to each of the marks, then brush away the chalk lines.

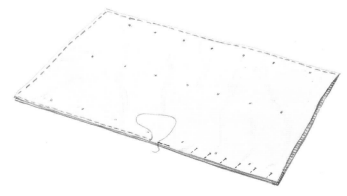

**3** With right sides together, pin the long side edges and top edge of the shade and the lining. Baste, then machine stitch, leaving a seam allowance of ¾ in (2 cm). Clip the corners, turn right side out, and press.

**4** Make a casing to hold the lath at the bottom of the shade on the same side as the rings. Press under a ¾-in (2-cm) fold along the raw edge, then press under a further 1¼-in (4-cm) fold. Baste, then machine stitch ⅛ in (3 mm) from the inside fold.

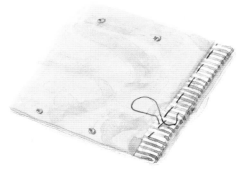

**5** Slip the lath inside the casing and use slipstitch to secure the open ends.

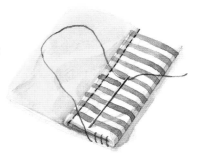

**6** If the shade is to fit in a recess, drill four equally spaced holes through the wooden strip from top to bottom. Mark the center back of the strip. Then secure the screw-eyes to the underside so one will lie at the top of each line of rings.

**7** Press a ¾-in (2-cm) fold to the wrong side along the shade's top edge. With the right side of the shade facing down, staple the centre top of the shade to the center back of the wooden strip, so the fold lies along the back edge of the strip. Continue stapling towards each end: the fabric will overlap the strip slightly.

**8** With the shade laid out flat and the rings uppermost, thread the cords in order from the shortest to the longest. Fasten a small safety pin to one end of the first cord. Thread the cord through the first screw-eye on the left, then down through the first line of rings. Undo the pin and sew the end of the cord securely to the final ring. Thread the second cord the same way, through the first and center screw-eyes, then through the center line of rings.

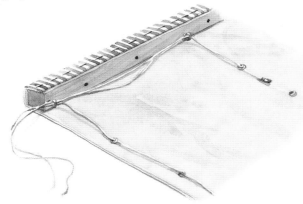

**9** Attach the third cord the same way, passing it through the preceding screw-eyes. Thread all the loose ends through the cord pull and adjust them so they are the same length. Knot securely, trim, and slide the cord pull over the knot. (For a shade that pulls up from the left, start with the first screw-eye on the right.)

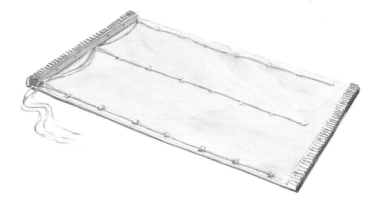

**10** A wall-mounted shade is mounted on or above the window frame, using a small angle bracket at each end of the strip. If the shade is to fit in a window recess, drill four holes in the top of the recess in line with the holes in the strip and use long screws and plugs to secure it in place. Screw a cleat on or near the frame, on the same side as the cords.

It is possible, given a large enough room, to have designated "ends" so that formal and informal areas are, to a certain extent, self-contained, with the appropriate window treatment used for each—say luxurious, swagged curtains at one window and a tailored shade, in the same fabric for continuity, at the other. Dividing curtains or a folding screen would reinforce the two-rooms-in-one approach without losing the feeling of space.

The other dual-purpose aspect of a living space is that it will probably be used with equal frequency during the day and night, so whatever fabric you opt for should be tested in both natural and artificial light before purchase. Similarly, the proposed style of curtain or shade should be assessed for its suitability both open and closed (or up and down).

Because many living rooms are at the front of the building, facing the street or public approach, how they look from the outside may be another consideration, for the rather dull rule that linings should be plain doesn't hold sway any longer, especially as more attractive alternatives—a stylish ticking, for instance—can be had at pretty much the same price.

**main picture** A tailored Roman shade is a chic and practical treatment for this window set above a daybed.

**left** Customizing these plain cream curtains with a boldly scalloped edge lifts them out of the ordinary and draws the eye to the view beyond.

**opposite, above right** Using one continuous pole with different-sized pairs of tailored drapes meets the challenges of this combination of French doors and side windows.

**opposite, below right** The contrasting band of paler (and more densely woven) fabric in these linen curtains makes an elegant statement and could be an inventive way to reinvent old curtains for a taller window.

# ribbon-trimmed lined curtains

These plain curtains have been transformed with an extravagant satin lining and velvet-ribbon trim. They are slightly too long so the folds spill onto the polished floor, increasing the feeling of opulence. The French pleats are created with a ready-made heading tape, but if you prefer a handmade finish, follow the method given on pages 59–61.

**MATERIALS AND EQUIPMENT**
plain fabric
contrasting satin lining
1-in (2.5-cm) and 3-in (8-cm) wide velvet ribbon
matching sewing thread
pencil
French-pleat heading tape
yardstick and carpenter's square
pronged curtain hooks
basic sewing kit

**MEASURING**
A = ½ length of curtain pole
B = from bottom of curtain rings to floor plus 5 in (13 cm)

**CUTTING OUT**
*curtain:*
width = 2 or 2.5 x A for each curtain, depending on the type of heading tape you have (refer to the manufacturer's instructions). Add to this 5 in (12 cm) for side hems plus 4 in (10 cm) for overlap
length = B plus 3 in (8 cm) for top hem plus 4 in (10 cm) for bottom hem

*lining:*
width = width of curtain panel minus 4 in (10 cm)
length = B minus 2½ in (6 cm)

*heading tape:*
A plus 10 in (25 cm)

**1** Mark the center top of the curtain and lining fabric with small notches.

**2** Press under a 1-in (2-cm) hem along the bottom of the lining.

**3** The ribbon edging runs along the sides and bottom of the curtain. Pin and baste the narrow ribbon 6 in (16 cm) in from the side edges and 10 in (25 cm) from the bottom, mitering the corners. Slipstitch by hand using matching sewing thread. Close the miters with slipstitch. Apply the wide ribbon in the same way, 4 in (10 cm) farther in.

**4** With right sides together and the top edges matching, pin and baste the sides of the curtain and lining. Starting at the top corners, machine stitch, leaving a seam allowance of ½ in (1 cm) to within 8 in (20 cm) of the bottom edge of the lining.

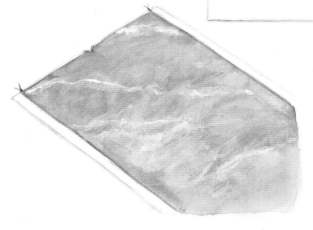

**5** Press the seam allowance lightly toward the center so it lies flat against the lining fabric, then turn right side out. Line up the notches on the top edge. Pin and baste from this point out to each corner. The seams will now lie 2 in (5 cm) in from the sides. Press the edges lightly.

**6** Press under a 3 in (8 cm) heading along the top edge. Turn the corners in at a slight angle and press.

**7** Gather up the heading tape to find out where the pinch pleats will form. Mark the position of the two outermost pleats with a pencil. Pull the heading tape flat again and lay it over the top hem. Adjust it so there is an equal space of approximately 4 in (10 cm) on each side of the outermost pleats, then pin it in place 1 in (2 cm) down from the top edge. Draw two lines across the tape to mark where it crosses the sides of the curtain.

**8** Unthread the gathering cords at each end of the tape to 2 in (4 cm) within the outer pencil line. On the leading edge, knot them securely together on the wrong side, and leave the other cords loose. Cut off the surplus tape along the lines, then press under ½ in (1 cm) to finish the ends. Baste, then machine stitch in place, starting each long row of stitching from the same end.

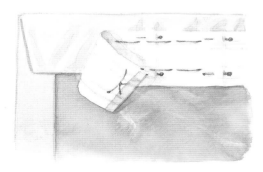

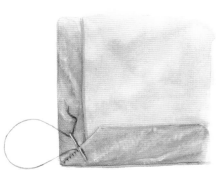

**9** Press under and unfold the remaining seam allowance along the sides of the lining, then unfold the hem. Miter each corner by turning in at a 45-degree angle so the crease lines match up. Press along the diagonal. Refold the hems, then slipstitch the miter. Baste the hem and the unstitched seam allowance at the sides.

**10** Double check the length, then press under a 4-in (10-cm) hem on the curtain. Miter as for the lining, then pin and baste the hem in place. Pin and baste the bottom edge of the lining onto the curtain and slipstitch in place.

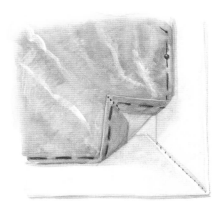

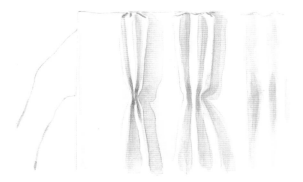

**11** Pull up the gathering cords to create the pleats. Rather than cut them, wrap the loose ends around a piece of cardboard, so the curtains can be flattened for drycleaning.

**12** Depending on the type of tape used, insert a curtain hook or a triple-pin hook at each pleat. To make sure that the three pleats hold together and give a crisper appearance, you can secure them at the base with a few small stitches.

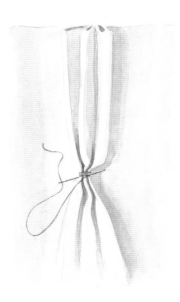

# KITCHENS

No longer placed firmly away out of sight, the kitchen is now at the heart of the home: the room where the family both cooks and eats, watches television and does homework, where everyone gathers for parties, and likely as not, where more money and thought has been spent than on any other home improvement, creating the "dream" kitchen which we all seem to hanker after.

This creates something of a dichotomy. If the kitchen is to be on show to all and sundry, then the curtains and shades need to keep up appearances, but as the kitchen is essentially a working room, filled with steam and cooking smells (which will cling to any fabrics present), the window treatment needs to be practical, too.

In fact, given that the kitchen is not usually a room where privacy is an issue, it may be that not all windows need a treatment at all, especially the small windows typically found above a counter or sink, which will be constantly splashed in any event. Similarly, it will probably be unnecessary, not to say unwise, to consider a layered window treatment.

Generally, lightly gathered curtains, café curtains, or simple, tailored shades are the obvious answer in a kitchen. For the fabrics, the best options will be washable, wipeable—oilcloth, for instance, makes great shades—or stain-resistant. Where the fabric will be washed—linen and cotton are, of course, ideal workhorse materials for kitchens—make allowance for any shrinkage, or preshrink the fabric before making the curtains.

Choose simple headings like tab-tops and tie-tops, and poles that can be easily dismantled for cleaning. You definitely want to avoid spending hours taking out and reinserting curtain hooks and adjusting decorative

The unusual striped fabric (combined with a coordinated linoleum floor) in this attractive dining-room-kitchen strikes the perfect balance between practicality and elegance for a working kitchen that is also used for entertaining. A shade above the countertop is a sensible choice, reproduced above the other window for continuity and balance. Using a single curtain at the French doors and anchoring it to the left of the doorway with a holdback keeps the fabric away from the counter.

headings when frequent laundering will be required. Plain or relatively unsophisticated fabrics will look more at ease with the working nature of the room than grand, ornately patterned ones and will better suit the simple style of the heading, too. And bear in mind that constant handling with sticky hands will soon leave a mark, so avoid curtain and shade styles that need lots of "coaxing" into position.

Don't forget to apply lateral thinking to the problem. Indeed, a winning solution may be right at hand in the shape of the humble dishtowel. Whether modern or antique, dishtowels make witty yet eminently sensible kitchen curtains and shades.

Where the kitchen is part of an open-plan living area, consider the solution that treats the room as two (or more) distinct areas linked by a common window-treatment theme. This may involve choosing the same patterned or solid fabric for all the windows, but adapting the styling of the window treatment to suit the function of each area—shades in the cooking area and gathered curtains in the

living area, for example. Here, choosing a fabric that is practical yet attractive enough to look the part sounds challenging, but good-quality natural fabrics like cottons and linens, either plain or in cheerful, timeless designs such as stripes, checks, plaids, or florals would fit the bill. And you can always add trimmings and other decorative details, such as an ornate pole or pair of finials, to the treatments in the living area if you feel the need to make things a bit more stylish.

**opposite, left** Wipeable floor-to-ceiling shades, decorated with rows of tiny holes, are a neat, flexible solution in a contemporary kitchen.

**opposite, above right** Curtains treatments have other uses in kitchens besides screening windows. Here, this simple plaid gathered panel hides the unsightly cleaning materials on an open shelf beneath the sink.

**opposite, below right** These lightly gathered gingham curtains are purely decorative. Attaching them to the window itself rather than the surrounding frame, means that the window can easily be opened for ventilation.

**this page** Loosely gathered, pencil-pleat curtains in an inexpensive, washable cotton cambric suit the country style of this open-plan kitchen-dining room.

**above** Nothing could be simpler, or more breezy, than these white cotton panels pinned up with curtain clips. They remain pristine because they are so easy to take down and launder.

**above right** Here, a whole length of dishtowel fabric—it was traditionally sold by the yard for housewives to make up into individual towels—makes an attractive Roman shade. Being of a simple, unstructured

construction, with no reinforcing poles, the blind can be gently hand-washed, cords and all.

**right** These fine linen curtains with integral valance are a prime example of how simple fabrics can be dressed up to offer a more sophisticated look for a dining area. They are not designed to be opened, but rather look sparkling clean and fresh while filtering the light in this sunny, all-white kitchen.

MATERIALS AND EQUIPMENT
cream linen
unbleached linen
matching sewing thread
sewing kit
curtain clips

MEASURING
A = width of window frame
B = length from bottom of pole
to windowsill

CUTTING OUT
*main panel:*
width = A plus 1 in (3 cm)
length = B plus 1 in (3 cm)

*short borders (cut 2):*
width = 3 in (8 cm)
length = A plus 1 in (3 cm)

*long borders (cut 2):*
width = 3 in (8 cm)
length = B plus 1 in (3 cm)

*ties (cut 7):*
width = 3 in (8 cm)
length = 86 in (70 cm)

# tie-top panel shade

This tie-top rectangular panel is the cheat's version of
a Roman shade, made without any rings or complicated
stringing. The pleats are held up at each side with
curtain clips; to let the shade down at night, simply
remove the clips. The ties and the narrow border are
made from the same fabric as the main shade, but in
a slightly darker shade.

**1** Press under a ½-in (1.5-cm)
allowance along one long
edge of each border strip.

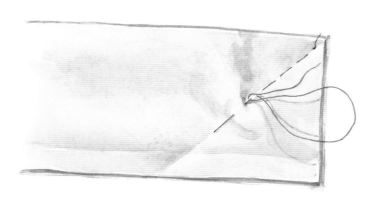

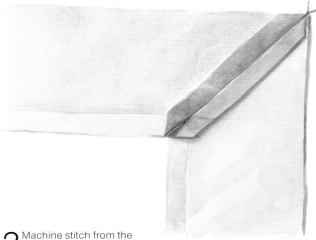

2 With right sides together and the creases matching, pin the ends of one short and one long border together. Fold the corner down to the edge opposite the crease to make a 45-degree angle and press lightly Baste along this crease with small stitches.

3 Machine stitch from the corner in, as far as the inner crease. Work a few extra stitches at each end to strengthen the seam. Trim the seam allowance to ½ in (1 cm), and press the seam open.

4 Join the remaining strips the same way. Lay the panel flat with the wrong side facing up. Place the frame over it with the right side facing down. Pin, baste, and machine stitch around the outside edge, leaving a ½-in (1.5-cm) seam allowance.

5 Clip and trim the corners so they will lie flat. Turn the frame to the other side, easing the corners into shape with a knitting needle, and press.

**6** Pin and baste the inside edge of the frame to the panel, then machine stitch down ⅛ in (3 mm) from the fold. Work a round of machine stitch ⅛ in (3 mm) from the outside edge.

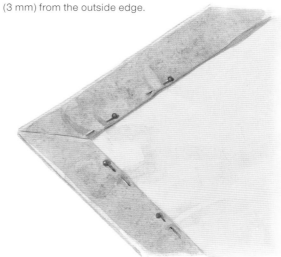

**7** To make the ties, press under a ⅝-in (1.5-cm) hem along each side. Fold in half lengthwise with wrong sides together, and pin and baste around the three open sides. Machine stitch, ⅛ in (3 mm) from the edge.

**8** Fold the ties in half. Pin, baste, and machine stitch the folds to the wrong side of the panel top at regular intervals.

**9** Knot the ties on the curtain rings. Fold up into pleats and fasten them in place with curtain clips.

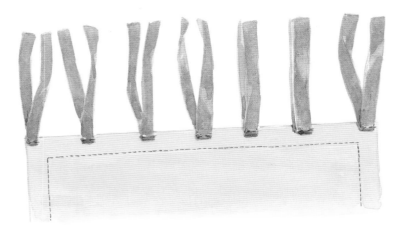

# BEDROOMS

Bedrooms are essentially private spaces; the nearest most of us come to having a personal sanctuary. Aspirations that they be calm and restful are universal, and here, perhaps more than in any other room, we are free—partners allowing—to give full rein to our personal flights of fancy, though this indulgence can lead to dangerous excesses.

Many bedrooms are relatively small, with the bed dominating the room and the remaining floor area taken up with storage. For this reason, be mindful when tempted to choose patterned fabric for curtains or shades. When these window treatments are combined with matching bedding, a modestly sized bedroom can easily seem like a sea of fabric.

To enhance the feeling of space, use a solid or subtly patterned, light-colored fabric—pale blues and greens are particularly soothing. Floor-length curtains will add height if the ceiling is low, but if space is at a premium, resist the temptation to make them heavily gathered or to allow them to puddle on the floor, because their bulk will

**opposite, above left** Light exclusion isn't a consideration in this all-white bedroom. Three-quarter-length voile curtains at the windows act as a pretty frame and link up with the curtain-as-headboard arrangement over the bed.

**opposite, above right** Lightweight patterned curtains suspended from the ceiling wrap this cocoonlike room.

**opposite, below left** Gilded antique valances lift these understated curtains above the ordinary.

**opposite, below right** Discreet, space-enhancing cream Roman shades team up with the luxury of a bed canopy and false bed hangings, adding a feeling of space to this small, but serene room.

**this page** It is perhaps fitting that vintage bed linen should find a new role as Roman shades in a bedroom. Interlining the blinds renders them lightproof.

**opposite** Not for the faint-hearted, this cotton jungle print used for curtains, the bed frame and a bolster shows that bedroom furnishings needn't look overtly feminine. Teamed with plain walls, white bed linen, and an understated carpet, the bold print is kept under control.

**this page** In stark contrast, these traditional-style, lined and interlined jacquard-weave curtains take a sedate role in this similarly toned interior. Sheer window shades allow for both light and privacy during the day.

visually and physically intrude into the room; at the very least, keep them in check with tiebacks.

The degree to which light needs to be blocked out depends on the individual; some of us would probably never wake up without the rallying help of daylight, but for others every chink of light needs to be excluded. To banish sunlight, use heavy, tightly woven fabrics, line and interline lighter ones, or use special blackout cloths (which aren't necessarily black), making sure that the curtain or shade is generous enough to overlap the edges of the window frame.

A layered treatment, such as sheers teamed with a blackout shade, is especially effective in a bedroom, accommodating several different levels of privacy and light exclusion: bedrooms aren't just used for sleeping in, after all, but often double as dressing rooms, home offices, and quiet spaces.

Where the bedroom does double as a study area, avoid overtly frilly or girlie fabrics and curtain styles that won't be conducive to getting down to work. Instead, bring those elements into the room with scatter cushions and throws that can be put away during the day.

1 Following the manufacturer's instructions and working outside or in a well-ventilated room, coat the fabric with stiffening spray. When dry, cut to size.

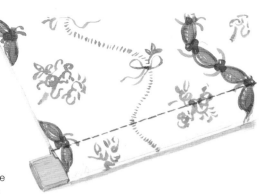

2 Press under a hem along the bottom to form a casing for the lath, then pin, baste, and machine stitch it down. The depth will depend on the size of the lath; check the guidelines supplied with the kit. Cut the lath ½ in (1 cm) shorter than the shade and slip it into the casing.

# floral shade

Often thought of as utilitarian and consigned to the kitchen or bathroom, plain shades can also be attractive and versatile. This floral shade provides a useful screen for a bedroom window, while the bobble-trimmed voile curtains are purely decorative. Kits containing all the components—along with comprehensive instructions—for making a shade are readily available from good furnishing suppliers.

3 Cut the doweling to size and hammer the second metal cap in place. Mark the midpoints of the rod and of the top of the fabric, then match the two together. Starting from the center and working out toward each end, staple the fabric to the doweling with the right side facing out.

**MATERIALS AND EQUIPMENT**
closely woven cotton fabric
stiffening spray
matching sewing thread
shade kit
hacksaw, hammer, and screwdriver
staple gun
basic sewing kit

**MEASURING AND CUTTING OUT**
*If blind is to hang inside a window recess:*
width = width of window recess minus ¾ in (2 cm)
length = from top of recess to sill plus 10 in (25 cm)

**IF BLIND IT TO HANG OUTSIDE A WINDOW RECESS OR OVER A FRAME:**
width = distance between molding
length = from top of frame to sill plus 10 in (25 cm)

4 Screw the fixtures in place and attach the shade as directed.

# ribbon embroidery

Plain white fabric with a loose square weave lends itself to extra embellishment. Here, long rows of basic running stitch have been embroidered down the length of the curtain using an assortment of colored ribbons to create a subtle striped effect.

MATERIALS AND EQUIPMENT
narrow ribbon
scissors
open-weave curtain
sewing needle
matching sewing thread
large tapestry needle

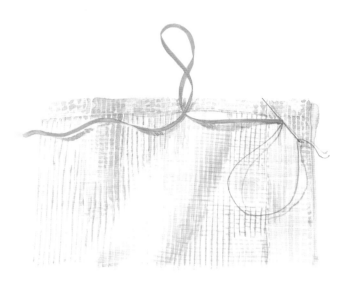

1 Cut a length of ribbon 5 in (12 cm) longer than the curtain and turn under ¼ in (5 mm) at one end. Sew the fold to the curtain just above the bottom edge, ½ in (1 cm) in from the side hem.

2 Thread the other end of the ribbon through a large tapestry needle. Work a row of evenly spaced running stitches about ½ in (1 cm) apart. Pull the ribbon up after every few stitches, keeping an even tension to prevent the fabric from distorting.

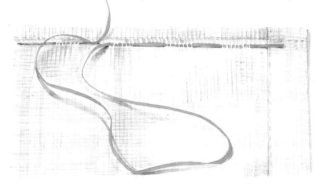

3 Continue sewing up to the top of the curtain. Trim the ribbon, fold under the end, and finish off with a few stitches.

4 Embroider the rest of the curtain the same way, alternating the colors and leaving 5-in (12-cm) spaces between the ribbons.

# CHILDREN'S ROOMS

The main thing to bear in mind when decorating a child's room is that his or her tastes will change very rapidly as they grow up. What appeals to a toddler now is likely to be deeply, deeply uncool just a few years down the line.

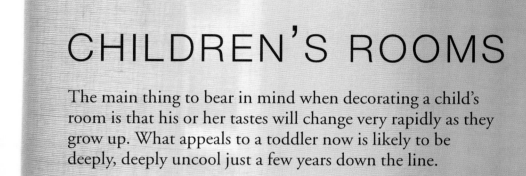

With this in mind, however tempting it is to indulge your child's (or your own) desire for pretty, pastel pinks and blues, or twee coordinated fabrics and wallpapers featuring nursery prints or cartoon characters, ask yourself do you really want, and can you afford, to change the scheme on a regular basis?

A safer option for expensive features like curtains and shades is to choose solid or simple cheery patterned fabrics, like checks, stripes, and dots in primary colors. Together with plain walls (which can easily and quickly be repainted as and when necessary), these should see children through to their teens. These sorts of fabrics have the additional benefit that they can be easily customized along the way with appliquéd panels for the curtains or themed borders for the walls.

opposite Checks and tiny flowers in navy and white would suit girls of any age, as well as younger boys. A multilayered treatment is flexible enough to adapt to different sleeping patterns.

this page If it weren't for the presence of the rocking horse, it would be difficult to guess the age of this bedroom's owner. The red and white checks and pretty florals make it child-friendly without being precious.

Children's bedrooms are the place to have fun with fabrics and furnishings. These simple cream curtains are given a groovy edge with multicolored tassels and would easily last a child through to the teenage years and beyond.

Alternatively, opt for decorative schemes that appeal to children of all ages and consequently won't fall out of favor too quickly. For example, a jaunty nautical look—easily achieved with blue and white stripes trimmed with rows of brightly colored pennants—or a jungle theme would be popular with kids of all ages.

In any event, with the inevitable accumulation of clothes, books, posters, stickers, and toys, a child's room will soon become subsumed by a riot of bright colors, so give in to the inevitable by installing plenty of shelf space to display toys and books, together with bulletin boards for posters and artwork, and provide furnishings that will offer a neutral background to this chaos. Before long, the room will be more than amply "decorated" to the child's individual style, and it will naturally evolve as their tastes and interests do.

On a practical note, especially with younger children and babies, establishing a bedtime routine will necessitate restricting daylight in the evenings

# tasseled curtain

Ready-made curtains and shades in neutral colors are widely available. This plain curtain has been customized with cotton tassels in bright primary colors to provide the perfect foil for the multicolored chaos of a child's bedroom.

MATERIALS AND EQUIPMENT
plain curtain
carpenter's square
yardstick
colored fine cotton yarn
thick cardboard
large-eyed needle
basic sewing kit

**1** Lay the curtain out flat, untying the cords if it has a gathered tape heading. Use a square to position the yardstick across the curtain 8 in (20 cm) down from the top edge.

**2** Starting 4 in (10 cm) from the edge, mark a row of points at 4 in (10 cm) intervals across the curtain. Move the ruler down a further 8 in (20 cm) and mark a second row, this time starting 8 in (20 cm) from the edge. Repeat these rows down to the hem.

**3** To make a tassel, wind the cotton yarn around a 4-in ( 10-cm) deep strip of cardboard ten times. Cut another length of yarn approximately 12 in (30 cm). Thread one end under the strands and tie tightly.

**4** Slip the loop off the cardboard. Bind one end of the yarn around the neck of the tassel to form a rounded top. Knot the two ends together, then cut through the loop and trim the tassel.

**5** Thread one end of the yarn through a large-eyed needle. Position the tassel over the a chalk mark and pass the needle through the curtain. If the curtain is lined, stitch to the main fabric only.

**6** Sew the other end of the yarn through the curtain ¼ in (5 mm) away so the tassel is held flat against the fabric. Knot the two ends together securely on the wrong side and clip.

**7** Make one tassel for each marked point, varying the colors so they are evenly scattered across the curtain. Regather the curtain, if necessary, and hang.

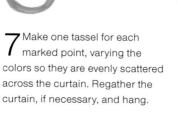

and mornings and for afternoon naps, so children's curtains need to be ultra-efficient at blocking out the light. Line and interline curtains; if you are using light-colored curtain fabric, consider using special blackout lining or, more flexibly, partnering the curtains with a blackout shade. Modern versions of blackout fabric aren't actually black and are specially designed to allow air to circulate through them.

Remember, too, that no matter how much care, thought—and money—is put into the furnishings you select, they are quite possibly likely to be vandalized with crayon and paint, regardless of whether or not paper is at hand, so make sure the curtain fabric can be washed and the shades are wipe-clean.

If you think your children might have mountaineering tendencies, it would be a good idea to make curtains sill-length rather than extending them to the floor. To minimize other possible injuries, avoid hard decorative details, such as metal holdbacks and bosses, or loose lengths of fabric, such as ribbon tiebacks, that could potentially choke a child.

**above** A mishmash of pretty, floral fabrics in blues and yellows looks cozy, without being cloying, while the frilly coronet above the bed would delight any aspiring princess.

**left** Pink may be viewed as a girlie shade, but the addition of a grown-up desk and some sophisticated pictures takes this pink and white scheme into adulthood.

**this picture** Essentially a plain white room, this nursery is 'decorated' for a child with the addition of sunny yellow curtains and a selection of toys.

# decorative panels

Ready-made curtains can be customized with panels of patterned fabric to make them look more interesting. In this child's bedroom, two color combinations of the same print have been used to upholster a low chair and to decorate the cream curtains. Each panel is edged with a different color braid, carefully chosen to blend with the material.

MATERIALS AND EQUIPMENT
plain unlined curtains
newspaper
printed fabric
woven braid in three colors
matching sewing thread
basic sewing kit

CUTTING OUT
Each curtain has two square- and one diamond-shaped panel. Cut out the shapes from newspaper and lay them on the curtain to determine the size and layout before cutting the fabric. (Untie the gathering cords first if the curtain has a tape heading.)

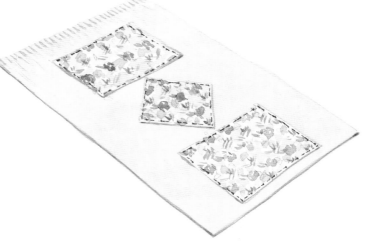

1 Lay the curtain out on the floor and place the three fabric panels in position. Pin and baste each one around the outside edge, making sure the fabric remains flat.

2 Turn the end of the first length of braid under at 45 degrees and pin it to one corner of the first panel. Pin it along all four sides, mitering each corner, then tuck under the other end to finish the seam. Baste in place.

3 Machine stitch along both sides of the braid, ⅛ in (3 mm) in from the edge. Sew both rows in the same direction so the braid does not pucker.

4 Edge the other two panels the same way and re-gather the heading, if necessary. Decorate the second curtain to make a matching pair.

# BATHROOMS

When you consider that bathrooms are invariably steamy and damp places where hygiene is the primary concern, it's a wonder we bring fabric into them at all; but we are creatures who seek comfort, and it is perhaps instinctive to wish to soften the starkness of hard surfaces like ceramic and enamel.

Since there is little we do in bathrooms that does not require the screening effects of a curtain or shade, it makes sense to have a solution that is in place all the time, and which perhaps works equally well for daytime and nighttime. Screens featuring decorative fretwork in the Arabian style would be both practical and effective. More flexible are plantation shutters—which are similar to louver shutters except that the slats are adjustable—and the obvious blind would be a Venetian one. They are available with either very narrow slats for a contemporary look or wider metal or wooden slats, ideal for larger windows.

For bathroom curtains, sheers are a sensible lightweight choice, but remember that electric light can render flat or lightly gathered sheer fabrics revealingly transparent at night, so unless you are prepared to use heavily gathered sheers—which will significantly reduce natural light during the day—you may have to fall back on a layered solution, say a plain neat shade teamed with lightly gathered curtains.

**opposite, above left** Here the window treatment in a traditional bathroom marries a practical Venetian blind with a decorative pleated shade. Using the same clean blue color for both unites what are disparate styles.

**opposite, above right** It is not normally necessary to exclude light completely in a bathroom, so a translucent shade is ideal, allowing some light in while preserving the modesty of the bather.

**opposite, below left** A London shade is a good compromise in a bathroom that could do with "softening" a little. This unstructured style looks elegant while being easily dismantled for cleaning.

**this page and opposite, below right** A Venetian blind is perfect for a bathroom, being endlessly adjustable to suit every requirement. By matching the color to the décor, it blends into the architecture.

Bathrooms, like kitchens, may be the place to break with the aesthetic rule that states curtains look better floor length. Sill-length curtains will prevent fabric from routinely sitting in wet puddles on the floor and may, in any event, be the only option where the basin or bathtub has been placed under the window.

Fabrics, if they are not to end up looking like limp rags, should be robust enough to withstand the inevitable steam. Sturdy linen, tightly woven cotton, or a plasticized fabric will do the job. Or, employing some lateral thinking, what about oilcloth or shower curtain fabric, which by necessity has to be waterproof, dampproof, and rotproof?

Other unusual solutions include variations on the beaded curtain. Consider making one using a variety of glass or plastic beads instead of the more traditional wooden type. Rust-resistant metal chain or lengths of ribbon weighed down with pretty objects are other interesting alternatives. Whatever solution you come up with, enlist a friend to verify that the window treatment is really as successful as you believe it to be!

**above** This over-length pewter-colored sheer makes a glamorous statement in a bathroom designed for luxurious relaxation. But note that such a thin fabric will only provide privacy during the day!

**right** A vintage Paco Rabanne dress of metal disks has been transformed into a curtain suspended from a sliding track. It provides privacy from the outside while allowing glimpses of the view for bathers looking out.

# ribbon and shell curtain

This alternative to the traditional bead curtain is an original way to display the results of a day's beachcombing. The shells are tied to translucent ribbons and hung from a bamboo pole. Search for scallops, clams, and limpets that have been worn by the sea, or hunt for abalones and other shells with natural holes.

MATERIALS AND EQUIPMENT

selection of ribbons in various widths

scissors

shells

bamboo stake the width of the window

awl

2 cup hooks

1 Cut a piece of ribbon to length, allowing an extra 6 in (15 cm) for the two knots. Choose a shell with a natural hole in it and thread one end of the ribbon through and tie tightly. Wrap the other end once around the stake ¾ in (2 cm) in from the end and knot in place.

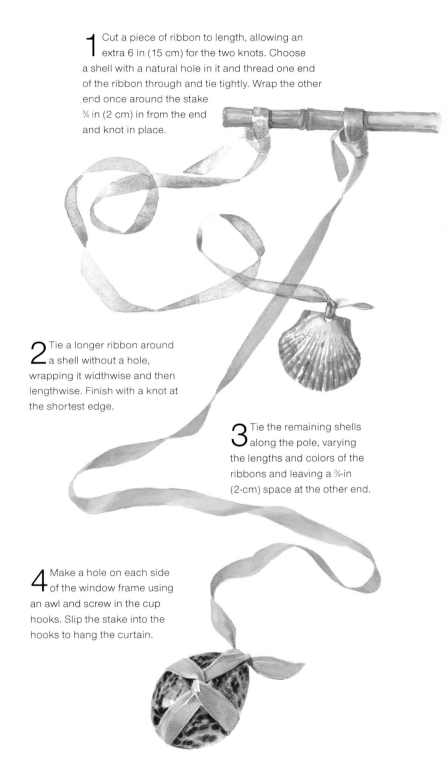

2 Tie a longer ribbon around a shell without a hole, wrapping it widthwise and then lengthwise. Finish with a knot at the shortest edge.

3 Tie the remaining shells along the pole, varying the lengths and colors of the ribbons and leaving a ¾-in (2-cm) space at the other end.

4 Make a hole on each side of the window frame using an awl and screw in the cup hooks. Slip the stake into the hooks to hang the curtain.

# PRACTICALITIES

## BASIC SEWING KIT

The equipment and techniques needed for the projects in this book are minimal, but it is worth investing in the best possible tools.

## Sewing machine

Modern sewing machines have many advanced stitching features, but most curtains require only a basic straight stitch and a zigzag for finishing raw edges. Always use a sharp needle and match its thickness to the weight of the fabric. The thinnest needles have the lowest numbers, so use size 8 for sheers, 12 for most projects, and size 16 for heavy canvas.

## Scissors

*Dressmaking shears* with long blades are used for cutting out and should be kept well sharpened. The handles are bent at an angle so you can cut accurately.

*Sewing scissors* are smaller and have straight handles. Use these for trimming seams and clipping corners.

*Embroidery scissors* have short, pointed blades, which make them ideal for trimming thread and notching seam allowances.

*Paper scissors* should be kept specially for cutting out patterns and templates.

## Needles

Hand-sewing needles come in various sizes for different tasks. Medium-length sharps are best for general sewing and basting, and shorter betweens can be used for slipstitch. Crewel needles have an extra-long eye designed for embroidery threads.

## Thimble

A flat-top metal thimble should be used to protect the fingers when basting heavy fabrics together, but it may take a while to get used to.

## Dressmaker's pins

These can be used for fine fabrics; larger glass-headed pins show up better on thicker material. Check that they are made from rustless steel.

## Sewing thread

Always choose a thread made from the same weight and fiber as the fabric being stitched. Mercerized cotton has a smooth surface and should be used for stitching cotton and linen. Polyester thread is finer and can be used for mixed fabrics. Match the color as closely as possible, and choose a darker shade if an exact match is not possible.

## Basting thread

The loosely spun thread used for basting is not mercerized, which means it breaks easily and can be unpicked without damaging a finished seam. Use a contrasting color that shows up well when basting stitches are being removed.

## Marking tools

*Tailor's chalk*, which comes in a thin, solid block, produces a fine line that brushes away easily. Use white for dark fabrics and the colored versions to mark paler cloth.

*Chalk pencils* can be sharpened to a fine point for detailed marking.

*Dressmaker's pens* have a water-soluble or light-sensitive ink that washes out or fades completely a few hours after use without leaving any marks.

## Iron

Hems and seams must be pressed well, so you need a good steam iron and a large ironing board. Use a cleaning cloth to remove any buildup.

## Measurements

Precise measurement is vital, so obtain a good tape measure that will not stretch with use and become inaccurate.

## CURTAIN FIXTURES

Poles, rods, and tracks contribute as much to the finished look of a window treatment as the curtains themselves; the two should complement each other, so give as much thought to choosing the fixtures as you do to the design and fabric.

Wood and metal poles are a decorative feature in themselves, often with ornate ends or finials, and are available in every style from a minimalist iron rod to baroque and classical reproductions. They are mounted on brackets screwed to the wall above the window. A heavy curtain will need a strong support, while lightweight sheers can be hung from a simple sprung rod, tension wire, or a length of curtain wire on cuphooks.

Tracks are concealed when the curtains are closed, and are often covered up with a

valance when the curtains are open. Some have a pull-cord system so the curtains can be opened and closed without handling them directly—this is ideal for delicate fabrics that can easily be damaged. Metal tracks should be used for thicker fabrics, and flexible tracks can be fitted into curved bay windows.

## MEASURING A WINDOW FOR CURTAINS

The curtain fixture should be in place before you start to measure. Allow enough overlap at each side of the window for the curtain to be pulled back: heavy curtains will require more wall space than sheers so they do not block too much light. Check that there is room for any tiebacks or holdbacks: you should position them after the curtains have been hung.

### Width [A]

For each curtain, take your measurement from the center of the window to the end of the pole, excluding the finial. If the track is made in two parts, allow 4 in (10 cm) or more extra for the overlap. Some metal fixtures have an angled return at each end, creating a corner to accommodate the fullness of the fabric when the curtains are pulled right back; add on this length if necessary.

### Length [B]

For full-length curtains, measure from the top edge of the track or the bottom of the rings down to the floor. If you want an extravagant look that spills onto the floor, add an extra 10 in (50 cm) or more to the finished length. Short curtains are measured to just below the sill, or to sill length if the window is deeply recessed.

## CUTTING OUT FABRIC

Press the fabric to remove any creases and lay it flat before cutting to the correct size. A large dining table is ideal, but a clean floor will work just as well. Cut off the selvages or clip into them at 4-in (10-cm) intervals (the edges of the fabric are often woven tightly and will distort the seams so the curtain will not drape properly).

Use a carpenter's square and a yardstick to mark the horizontal cutting lines at right angles to the sides. If your fabric has a loose weave, you may be able to pull out a weft thread across the width to mark the line. Label the top edge of each piece: even solid fabrics may have variations in the weave that will reflect the light differently.

## JOINING FABRIC WIDTHS

A center seam can look awkward—particularly on a shade—so if the panel has two drops, cut one of them in half. Sew the two narrow pieces to the outside edges.

## WORKING WITH PATTERNED FABRICS

Any fabrics with a pattern—from small-scale checks to floral prints—must be matched when two or more drops are joined to create the required width, and also across both curtains to make a pair. Measure the depth of the pattern repeat and add it onto each length when calculating the amount of fabric needed. When cutting out the panels, make sure the top edge of each drop starts at the same point on the design.

The lengths should be joined so the design matches horizontally across the seam line. Press under the seam allowance on the first length and place it over the second, adjusting it so the patterns match exactly. Pin close to the fold, then baste the seam allowances together on the wrong side. Machine stitch along the crease line.

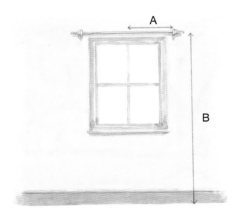

MEASURING A WINDOW FOR CURTAINS

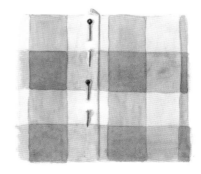

JOINING PATTERNED FABRIC

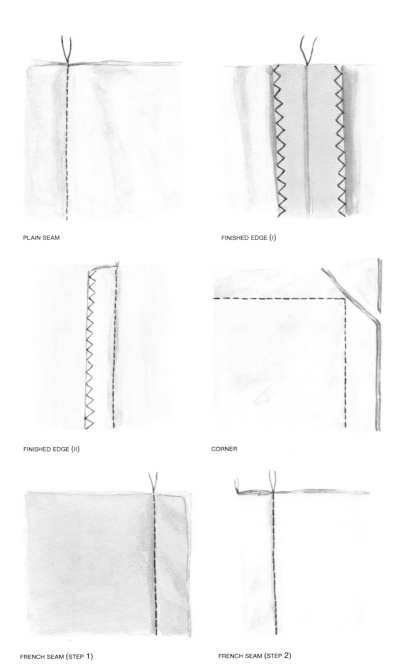

PLAIN SEAM

FINISHED EDGE (I)

FINISHED EDGE (II)

CORNER

FRENCH SEAM (STEP 1)

FRENCH SEAM (STEP 2)

## SEAMS

The extra fabric needed to join two pieces of fabric is called the seam allowance. To keep it consistent, match the raw edges to the corresponding line on the bed of the sewing machine when stitching.

### Plain seam

Line up the two raw edges with right sides together. Pin together at intervals of 2–4 in (5–10 cm), inserting the pins at right angles to the fabric or parallel to the edge. Baste, then machine stitch along the seam line. Press the seam open or to one side as directed and remove the basting.

### Finished edge

The cut edge of a plain seam may fray, especially if an item is washed. To prevent this, a line of zigzag or overlock stitch can be worked along each raw edge before seaming if the seam is to be pressed open (i). If the seam is to be pressed to one side, the seam allowance can be trimmed and the two edges joined together with a zigzag (ii).

### Corner

To sew around a right-angled corner, stitch to the end of the seam allowance. Lift the presser foot, leaving the needle down. Turn the fabric through 90 degrees, and continue stitching. Clip off the corner to within ¹⁄₁₆ in ( 2 mm) of the stitching before turning through, so it will lie flat.

### French seam

Used for joining lightweight or sheer fabrics, this seam encloses the raw edges on the wrong side. With wrong sides together, seam the fabric ⅜ in ( 8 mm) from the edge. Trim the allowance to ¼ in ( 6 mm) and fold the right sides together. Stitch again, ⅜ in ( 8 mm) from the edge.

## HEMS

The finish to the lower edge of a piece of fabric depends on its weight:

### Single hem

Used for heavier linen and upholstery fabrics. Zigzag the raw edge
and press the hem up to the required length on the wrong side.
Pin and baste, then sew in place by hand, or machine stitch just
below the zigzag.

SINGLE HEM

### Double hem

Consists of one narrow and one deeper turning or two equal turnings,
which give a firmer edge to finer fabrics. Press under ¼ in (6 mm)
along the raw edge, then turn up to length as directed. Pin and baste,
then either machine stitch close to the inner fold, or finish by hand
for a neater result.

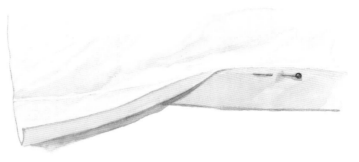

DOUBLE HEM

## HAND STITCHING

The majority of the sewing for all the projects in this book is stitched
by machine, but hand sewing is vital for basting and finishing off
hems, miters, and some seams.

### Slipstitch

Used to join two folded edges or to secure a folded hem. Bring the
needle out through the fold and pick up two threads of the other
fabric. Pass the needle back through the fold for 6 mm (¼ in) and
repeat to the end.

SLIPSTITCH                    HERRINGBONE STITCH

### Herringbone stitch

Creates a flat, unobtrusive hem for curtains. Bring the needle up
inside the hem and make a diagonal stitch up to the right, then a short
horizontal stitch to the left. Work a diagonal stitch down to the right
and, taking the needle through the top layer of the hem, make a short
horizontal stitch to the left. Repeat these two stitches to continue.

# RESOURCES

## GENERAL SUPPLIERS

**ABC Carpet & Home**
888 Broadway
New York, NY 10003
(212) 473-3000
www.abchome.com
*Retailer of fabrics, furniture, bed linens, all home products.*

**Ballard Designs**
1670 Defoor Avenue, NW
Atlanta, GA 30318
(800) 367-2775
www.ballarddesigns.com
*Retailer. Catalog selling furniture, fabrics, lampshades; custom workroom.*

**Bed Bath & Beyond**
620 Avenue of the Americas
New York, NY 10011
(212) 255-3550
*Home superstore, including window treatments.*

**Bloomingdales**
1000 Third Avenue
New York, NY 10022
(212) 705-2000
www.bloomingdales.com
*Department stores with decorating departments.*

**Crate and Barrel**
(800) 967-6696
www.crateandbarrel.com
*Retailer, catalog. Furniture and accessories.*

**Home Depot**
*A wide selection of hardware. Check local telephone directory for the store nearest you.*

**Macy's**
(800) BUY-MACY
www.macys.com
*Department stores nationwide.*

**Nieman Marcus**
(800) 825-8000
www.neimanmarcus.com
*Department stores and catalog.*

**Pottery Barn**
(800) 838-0944
www.potterybarn.com
*Retailer of furniture and accessories. Stores nationwide. Catalog.*

## FABRICS

**Anichini**
(800) 553-5309
www.anichini.com
*Manufacturer of fabrics and home furnishings.*

**B & J Fabrics**
263 West 40th Street
New York, NY 10018
(212) 354-8150
*Local retailer. Natural-fiber fabrics. Search and special-order services.*

**Baranzelli Home**
1127 Second Avenue
New York, NY 10022
(212) 753-6511
*Local retailer. High-quality fabric and trimmings.*

**Bechenstein's Home Fabrics**
4 West 20th Street
New York, NY 10011
(212) 366-5142
*Local retailer.*

**Boussac Fedini, Inc.**
979 Third Avenue
New York, NY 10022
(212) 421-0534
*Italian silks, tissued taffetas, cotton printed and woven fabrics with coordinating wallcoverings. To trade only.*

**Brunschwig & Fils**
979 Third Avenue
New York, NY 10022
(212) 838-7878
www.brunschwig.com
*Fabrics and furniture sold to the trade. 19 showrooms worldwide.*

**Calico Corners**
(800) 213-6366
www.calicocorners.com
*Fabric from manufacturers such as Waverly, Ralph Lauren. Many stores nationwide.*

**Clarence House Imports**
211 East 58th Street
New York, NY 10022
(212) 752-2890
(800) 632-0076
www.clarencehouse.com
*Printed natural-fiber fabrics based on documents from the 15th–20th centuries. Hand-woven textiles. To trade only.*

**Covington Fabrics**
15 East 26th Street
New York, NY 10010
(212) 689-2200
*Classic and fashion-forward fabrics. To trade only.*

**Cowtan & Tout, Inc.**
979 Third Avenue
New York, NY 10022
(212) 753-4488
*Traditional fabrics to trade, from silk brocades to prints on linen.*

**Donghia Home Furnishings**
979 Third Avenue
New York, NY 10022
(800) DONGHIA
www.donghia.com
*Fabrics and furniture to trade. Showrooms nationwide.*

**The Fabric Center**
485 Electric Avenue
Fitchburg, MA 01420
(978) 343-4402
*A wide variety of decorator fabrics at discounted prices. Mail order. Catalog.*

**Hinson & Co.**
979 Third Avenue
New York, NY 10022
(212) 688-5538
*Fabrics with an emphasis on clean designs. Also coordinating wall-coverings and decorative accessories and trims. To trade only.*

**Keepsake Quilting**
Route 25B
P.O. Box 1618
Center Harbor
NH 03226-1618
(800) 865-9458
www.keepsakequilting.com
*Lightweight cottons. There is also a wide range of threads and notions available. Mail order. Catalog.*

**Inter-Coastal Textile**
480 Broadway
New York, NY 10013
*Retailer of decorative fabrics at a discount.*

**Oppenheim's**
P.O. Box 29
120 East Main Street
North Manchester
IN 46962-0052
(800) 461-6728
*Retailer. Country prints, denim, chambray, flannel fabrics, and mill remnants.*

**Pierre Deux**
870 Madison Avenue
New York, NY 10021
(212) 570-9343
(800) 774-3773
www.pierredeux.com
*French printed fabrics. Custom drapery service. Unique trims. Mail order. Catalog.*

**Quinns Essentials**
19 East Cross Street
Ypsilanti, MI 48198
(734) 544-4690
(877) 7-QUINNS
www.quinnsessentials.com
*Large selection of name-brand fabrics. Interior design studio.*

**Rose Brand**
75 Ninth Avenue, 4th Floor
New York, NY 10011
(212) 242-7554
www.rosebrand.com
*Theatrical fabrics, custom draperies, muslins, wide widths, sheers, netting, tulle, and some trimmings.*

**F. Schumacher & Co.**
79 Madison Avenue
New York, NY 10016
(212) 213-7900
(800) 523-1200
www.fschumacher.com
*Extensive selection of fabrics in various fibers. Also coordinating trims available. To trade only.*

**Scalamandre Silk, Inc.**
942 Third Avenue
New York, NY 10022
(212) 980-3888
(800) 932-4361
*Restorer of classic document fabrics for historic houses, with adaptations available for home use. Trims, wallpaper, custom carpets. Also houses Museum of Textiles. To trade only.*

**Silk Trading Co.**
360 South La Brea Avenue
Los Angeles, CA 90036
(800) 854-0396
www.silktrading.com
*Retailer and catalog. More than 2,000 silk fabrics, from taffeta to classic damask, ready-made curtains, trimmings, lampshades. Nine stores nationwide.*

Thai Silks!
252 State Street
Los Altos, CA 94022
(800) 722-7455
www.thaisilks.com
*Silk, velvet, organza, jacquard, taffeta. Mail order. Catalog.*

Waverley Fabrics
79 Madison Avenue
New York, NY 10016
(212) 213-7900
(800) 523-1200
www.waverly.com
*Printed and woven fabrics, coordinating accessories and wallpaper borders. To trade only.*

Pauline Yeats
26 East 22nd Street
New York, NY 10003
(212) 228-5353
*Retailer of designer furniture and fabrics.*

## CURTAIN HARDWARE

American Steel Window Service
108 West 17th Street
New York, NY 10011
(212) 242-8131
*Vintage window hardware.*

Kirsch
P.O. Box 0370
Sturgis, MI 49091
(800) 528-1407
*Manufacturer of curtain and drapery hardware and rods.*

Levolor Home Fashions
309 N. Prospect Street
Sturgis, MI 49091
(800) 528-1407
www.levolor.com
*Shades, hardware and rods.*

Materials Unlimited
2 West Michigan Avenue
Ypsilanti, MI 48197
800 299 9462
*Antique and reproduction hardware.*

Renovators Supply
San Francisco, CA 94117
415-563-2727
*Drapery hardware.*

Rollease, Inc.
200 Harvard Avenue
Stamford, CT 06902
(203) 964-1573
(800) 552-5100
www.rollease.com
*One-cord control system for blinds and shades. Mail order. Catalog.*

Rue de France
78 Thomas Street
Newport, RI 02840
(401) 846-3636
(800) 777-0998
www.ruedefrance.com
*All types of hardware and a selection of fabric curtains and accessories. Mail order. Catalog.*

## CURTAINS AND SHADES

Martin Albert Interiors
9 East 19th Street
New York, NY 10003
(212) 673-8000
*To the trade. Custom window treatments, upholstery, fabric.*

All State Glass Corp.
85 Kenmare Street
New York, NY 10012
(212) 226-2517
www.allstateglasscorp.com
*Shades and blinds.*

Country Curtains
The Red Lion Inn
Stockbridge, MA 01262
(413) 298-5565
(800) 876-6123
www.countrycurtains.com
*Fabric and lace curtains, swags, hardware and other accessories. Stores mostly in east of the U.S.A. Mail-order catalog.*

Harry Zarin
292 Grand Street
New York, NY 10002
(212) 925-6112
www.harryzarin.com
*Discount large selection fabrics, blinds and shades*

Hunter Douglas
One Duette Way
Broomfield, CO 80020
(888) 501-8364
www.hunterdouglas.com
*Manufacturer of all kinds of shades and window treatments.*

Smith & Noble
P.O. Box 1387
Corona, CA 91718
(800) 560-0027
www.smithandnoble.com
*Retailer, catalog. All kinds of shades and window treatments.*

Springs Window Fashions
7549 Graber Road
Middleton, WI 53562
800 521 8071
www.springs.com
*Vinyl, metal, and fabric vertical and horizontal blinds and shades. Fashion and pleated shades. Mail order. Catalog.*

Sundial & Schwartz
159 East 118th Street
New York, NY 10035
(212) 289-4969
www.sundial.baweb.com
*Mirroring and window treatments, blinds, shades and draperies.*

The Warm Co.
954 East Union
Seattle, WA 98122
(800) 234-9276
*Manufacturer of insulated fabric for window shades.*

www.shadeambition.com
Davis, CA
(800) 838-5442
*Manufacturer and online retailer of minishades.*

## NOTIONS AND TRIMMINGS

Clothilde Inc.
2 Sew Smart Way
Stevens Point
WI 54481-8031
(800) 772-2891
*Retailer of discounted notions, trims, and threads.*

Conso Products
P.O. Box 326
Union, SC 29379
(800) 845-2431
www.conso.com
*Manufacturer of decorative trims, tassels, and fringes.*

Hollywood Trims
Prym-Dritz Corp.
P.O. Box 5028
Spartanburg, SC 29304
(800) 845-4948
www.prymdritz.com
*Manufacturer of rayon, cotton, and metallic trims, cords, tassels, and thread.*

Houlés, Inc.
8584 Melrose Avenue
Los Angeles, CA 90069
(310) 652-6171
*Luxurious handmade imported trimmings. Hardware. To trade only. Showrooms nationwide.*

Clotilde, Inc.
B 3000
Louisiana, MO 63353
(800) 772-2891
www.clotilde.com
*Discounted notions, trims, and threads. Mail order. Catalog.*

French General
35 Crosby Street
New York, NY 10012
(212) 343-7474
frenchgeneral.com
*Vintage notions, ribbon, velvet leaves and flowers, glass garlands, and decor items from French flea markets.*

Gelberg Braid Co.
243 West 39th Street
New York, NY 10018
(212) 730-1121
www.gelbergbraid.com
*Manufacturer of trimming.*

K. Trimming Co.
519 Broadway
New York, NY 10012
(212) 431-8929
*Incredible collection of notions and trimmings.*

Lou Lou Buttons
69 West 38th Street
New York, NY 10018
(212) 398 5498
*Local retailer.*

Metropolitan Impex
966 Avenue of the Americas
New York, NY 10018
(212) 502 5243
www.metropolitanimpex.com
*Good selection of trimmings, feathers, laces and beads.*

Nancy's Notions
P.O. Box 683
Beaver Dam, WI 53916
(800) 833-0690
www.nancysnotions.com
*Notions, trims, threads, books, and videos for the home sewer. Mail order. Catalog.*

C. M. Offray & Sons, Inc.
Route 24
P. O. Box 601
Chester, NJ 07930
(908) 879-4700
www.offray.com
*Woven and wire-edge ribbons, flowers, and bows. From fabric and notion stores nationwide.*

Penn & Fletcher
21-07 41st Avenue, 5th Floor
New York, NY 11101
(212) 239 6868
www.pennandfletcher.com
*Quality trims and lace, beading and embroidery service.*

## ARCHITECTS AND DESIGNERS WHOSE WORK IS FEATURED IN THIS BOOK

Key: a=above, b=below, c=centre l=left, r=right.

**Nicholas Arbuthnott**
Arbuthnott Ladenbury
Architects
Architects & Urban Designers
15 Gosditch Street
Cirencester GL7 2AG, UK
**Vanessa Arbuthnott Fabrics**
The Tallet
Calmsden
Cirencester GL7 5ET, UK
www.vanessaarbuthnott.co.uk
**Country House Walks Ltd**
Self-catering accommodation/
weekend breaks
The Tallet
Calmsden
Cirencester GL7 5ET, UK
www.thetallet.co.uk
*Page 16r.*

**Andrew Arnott and Karin Shack**
Art & Design
517 High Street
Prahran
Victoria 3181
Australia
*Page 17r.*

**Ash Sakula Architects**
24 Rosebery Avenue
London EC1R 4SX, UK
t. +44 20 7837 9735
f. +44 20 7837 9708
robert@ashsak.com
www.ashsak.com
*Page 57r.*

**Azman Owens**
Architects
8 St Albans Place
London NW1 0NX, UK
t. +44 20 7354 2955
f. +44 20 7354 2966
*Page 4.*

**James Biber, AIA**
Pentagram Architecture
204 Fifth Avenue
New York, New York 10010
*Page 30bl.*

**Blakes Lodging**
77 Pantigo Road
East Hampton
New York NY 11937
t. 631 324 1815
jeblake@suffolk.lib.ny.us
www.picket.com/blakesBB/blak
es.htm
*Pages 40b, 94.*

**Laura Bohn Design Associates**
30 West 26th Street
11th floor
New York NY 10010
t. 212 645 3636
f. 212 645 3639
www.laurabohndesign.com
*Page 14r.*

**Nancy Braithwaite Interiors**
2300 Peachtree Road
Suite C101
Atlanta
Georgia 30309
*Pages 5, 83bl, 115, 130al.*

**Sabina Fay Braxton**
Cloth of Gold
Grennan Watermill
Thomastown
Co Kilkenny
Ireland
t. +353 565 4383
f. +353 565 4384
by appointment in New York:
t. 212 535 2587
by appointment in Paris:
t. +33 1 46 57 11 62
cofgold@indigo.ie
*Pages 12br, 20 both, 67cr.*

**Carden Cunietti**
83 Westbourne Park Road,
London W2 5QH, UK
t. office +44 20 7229 8559
t. shop +44 20 7229 8630
f. +44 20 7229 8799
cc@carden-cunietti.com
www.carden-cunietti.com
*Pages 7l, 10bl, 11, 22ar, 32, 75, 80, 106–107, 109, 130ar, 130bl, 132l, 138, endpapers.*

**Marisa Tadiotto Cavalli**
Via Solferino, 11
20121 Milano
Italy
t. +39 03 48 41 01 738
   +39 02 86 46 24 26
f. +39 02 29 00 18 60
marisscavalli@hotmail.com
*Pages 22al, 23, 68ar.*

**Sian Colley Soft Furnishings**
Block E, 2B Upper Ringway
Bounds Green,
London N11 2UD, UK
t./f +44 20 8368 4092
colleysian@hotmail.com
*Pages 12a, 12bl, 56, 88, 99c, 99b, 101cr, 104–105, 105a, 113.*

**CR Studio Architects, PC**
6 West 18th Street, 9th floor
New York NY 10011
t. 212 989 8187
f. 212 924 4282
victoria@crstudio.com
www.crstudio.com
*Page 118ar.*

**Charlotte Crosland Interiors**
62 St Mark's Road
London W10 6NN, UK
t.+44 20 8960 9442
f. +44 20 8960 9714
mail@charlottecosland.com
www.charlottecrosland.com
*Pages 2, 7c, 17c, 96–97, 98, 98–99, 99a, 105b, 110, 111, 118br, 119.*

**Vincent Dané**
Interior Design Antiques
50 Cranby Gardens
London SW7 3DE, UK
*Pages 34, 63br, 112br.*

**Eric De Queker**
DQ Design In Motion
Koninklijkelaan 44
2600 Bercham
Belgium
*Pages 24bl, 30br.*

**Mary Drysdale**
1733 Connecticut Avenue NW
Washington DC 20009
*Page 35.*

**Christian de Falbe Interior Design**
The Glasshouse
49a Goldhawk Road
London W12 8QP, UK
t. +44 20 8743 3210
f. +44 20 8746 7602
studio@cdef.co.uk
www.cdef.co.uk
*Pages 10ar, 21ac, 21b, 26, 27, 74all, 87a.*

**Fiil & Co**
Designers of curtain panels and
home interiors & accessories
amfiil@c.dk
Shop:
Lavender Hill
Østergade 24B
1100 Copenhagen K, Denmark
t. +45 33 121201
f. +45 33 121701
*Pages 8–9, 10br, 42r both, 68br, 69 main, 69 inset left, 70–71.*

**Gloss Ltd**
Designers of home accessories
274 Portobello Road
London W10 5TE, UK
t. +44 20 8960 4146
f. +44 20 89604842
pascale@glossltd.u-net.com
*Page 78bl.*

**Russell Glover**
Architect
russellglover@earthlink.net
*Page 75acr.*

**Christophe Gollut**
Alistair Colvin Limited
116 Fulham Road
London SW3 6HU, UK
*Pages 21ar, 50r.*

**Mark Guard Architects**
161 Whitfield Street
London W1P 5RY, UK
020 7380 1199
*Page 25.*

**Yves Halard**
Interior Decoration
27 Quai de la Tournelle
75005 Paris
France
t. +33 1 4407 14 00
f. +33 1 44 07 1030
*Pages 63a*

**Wendy Harrop**
Interior Designer
11 Rectory Road
London SW13 0DU, UK
*Pages 41al, 42al.*

**Kelly Hoppen Interiors**
2 Alma Studios
32 Stratford Road
Kensington
London W8 6QF, UK
*Page 29.*

**Hotel Villa Gallici**
Aix en Provence
France
*Pages 59, 61.*

**Interni Pty Ltd.**
Interior Design Consultancy
15–19 Boundary Street
Rushcutter's Bay
Sydney 2010
Australia
*Page 51a.*

**Malin Iovino Design**
t. +44 20 7252 3542
f. +44 20 7252 3542
iovino@btinternet.com
*Page 112l.*

**IPL Interiors**
Thames House- Unit 26Cl
140 Battersea Park Road
London SW11 4NY, UK
t. +44 20 7622 3009
f. +44 20 7622 2246
ipl.interiors@virgin.net
*Pages 17l, 36–39, 91ar, 120,*
*121, 124, 130br, 131.*

**Janie Jackson**
Stylist/Designer
Parma Lilac
Children's nursery furnishings &
accessories
t. +44 20 8960 9239
*Page 24ar.*

**Jacomini Interior Design**
1701 Brun, Suite 101
Houston
Texas 77019
*Pages 40a, 70.*

**Daniel Jasiak**
Designer
12 rue Jean Ferrandi
Paris 75006
France
t. +33 1 45 49 13 56
f. +33 1 45 49 23 66
*Page 14l.*

**Johnson Naylor**
13 Britton Street
London EC1M 5SX, UK
t. +44 20 7490 8885
f. +44 20 7490 0038
brian.johnson@johnsonnaylor.co.uk
*Page 67ar.*

**Khai Liew Design**
166 Magill Road
Norwood
South Australia 5067
*Page 91al.*

**Bruno & Hélène Lafforgue**
Mas de l'Ange
Maison d'Hôte
Petite route de St. Remy-de-
Provence
13946 Mollégès
France
*Page 41ar.*

**Larcombe & Solomon**
**Architects**
Level 3, 397 Riley Street
Surry Hills 2010
NSW
Australia
*Page 63bc.*

**Nicoletta Marazza**
Via G Morone, 8
20121 Milan
Italy
t/f +39 2 7601 4482
*Page 101l.*

**Jeff McKay Inc.**
Advertising and Public Relations
Agency
203 Lafayette Street
New York NY 10012
t. 212 771 1770
*Page 132r.*

**Frédéric Méchiche**
4 rue de Thorigny
75003 Paris
France
*Pages 41br, 86al, 86bl.*

**Mullman Seidman Architects**
Architecture & interior design
443 Greenwich Street # 2A
New York NY 10013
t. 212 431 0770
f. 212 431 8428
msa@mullmanseidman.com
www.mullmanseidman.com
*Page 65.*

**Roger Oates Design**
Shop & Showroom:
1 Munro Terrace
off Cheyne Walk
Chelsea
London SW10 0DL, UK
Studio Shop:
The Long Barn
Eastnor
Ledbury
Herefordshire HR8 1EL, UK
Rugs and Runners Mail Order
Catalogue:
t. +44 1531 631611
*Page 101br.*

**Ogawa/Depardon Architects**
Architects
137 Varick Street, #404
New York NY 10013
t. 212 627 7390
f. 212 627 9681
ogawdep@aol.com
*Page 81.*

**OKA Direct**
A unique collection of mail-order
furniture and accessories for the
home including rattan, painted
furniture, leather and horn. For a
catalogue please call +44 870
160 6002
www.okadirect.com
*Page 21al.*

**Andrew Parr**
SJB Interior Design Pty Ltd.
Studio Southbank
5 Haig Street
South Melbourne 3205,
Australia
*Page 51b.*

**Campion A. Platt**
641 Fifth Avenue
New York, NY 10022
*Pages 28–29.*

**Géraldine Prieur**
Interior Designer
7 rue Faraday
75017 Paris
France
t. +33 1 44 40 29 12
f. +33 1 44 40 29 17
*Page 15.*

**Lena Proudlock**
Denim in Style
Drews House
Leighterton
Gloucestershire GL8 8UN, UK
t/f. +44 1666 890230
*Page 63bl.*

**Reed Creative Services Ltd**
151a Sydney Street
London SW3 6NT, UK
t. +44 20 7565 0066
f. +44 20 7565 0067
*Page 50al.*

**Johanne Riss**
Stylist, designer & fashion
designer
35 Place du Nouveau Marché
aux Graens
1000 Brussels
Belgium
t. +32 2 513 0900
f. +32 2 514 3284
*Page 67br.*

**Steven Roxburghe Designs**
48 Kensington Church Street
London W8 4DA, UK
t./f. +44 20 7937 0051
steven.roxburghe@virgin.net
*Pages 28, 33all, 143.*

**Charles Rutherfoord**
51 The Chase
London SW4 0NP, UK
*Page 62.*

**Sheila Scholes**
Designer
t. +44 1480 498 241
*Pages 6, 48, 71, 83al, 84, 85, 92,*
*100, 140, 144.*

**Sequana**
64 Avenue de la Motte Picquet
75015 Paris
France
t. +33 1 45 66 58 40
f. +33 1 45 67 99 81
sequana@wanadoo.fr
*Page 57bl.*

**Enrica Stabile**
Antiques Dealer, interior
decorator & photographic stylist
L'Utile e il dilettevole
Via della Spiga, 46
Milan
Italy
t. +39 02 76 00 84 20
e.stabile@enricastaile.com
www.enricastabile.com
*Pages 58al, 112ar, 128a.*

**Todhunter Earle Interiors**
Interior Design Company-
undertake a wide variety of
projects, based in Chelsea.
Chelsea Reach, 1st Floor
79–89 Lots Road
London SW10 0RN, UK
t. +44 20 7349 9999
f. +44 20 7349 0410
interiors@todhunterearle.com
www.todhunterearle.com
*Pages 1, 52, 53, 55, 83ar, 87b,*
*118bl, 125, 128bl.*

**Sasha Waddell**
269 Wandsworth Bridge Road
London SW6 2TX, UK
t. +44 20 7736 0766
*Pages 13, 31b, 122.*

**Vicente Wolf Associates, Inc.**
333 West 39th Street
New York, NY 10018
*Page 101ar.*

# Picture Credits

All illustrations by Lizzie Sanders, all photographs by Polly Eltes unless specified otherwise.

Key: ph=photographer, a=above, b=below, c=center, l=left, r=right.

Endpapers Debby & Jeremy Amias' house in London designed by Carden Cunietti; 1 Emily Todhunter's house in London designed by Todhunter Earle Interiors; 2 A house in London designed by Charlotte Crosland Interiors; 4 ph Andrew Wood/Guido Palau's house in North London, designed by Azman Owens Architects; 5 ph Simon Upton; 6 Sheila Scholes' house near Cambridge; 7l Debby & Jeremy Amias' house in London designed by Carden Cunietti; 7c A house in London designed by Charlotte Crosland Interiors; 7r ph James Merrell/Sue and Andy A'Court; 8–9 Anne-Mette Fiil's house near Cambridge; 10al ph James Merrell/fabric from Ian Mankin; 10ar Christian de Falbe's London home; 10bl Debby & Jeremy Amias' house in London designed by Carden Cunietti; 10br Anne-Mette Fiil's house near Cambridge; 11 Debby & Jeremy Amias' house in London designed by Carden Cunietti; 12a&bl Curtain design by Sian and Annie Colley; 12br ph David Montgomery/Sabina Fay Braxton's apartment in Paris; 13 ph David Montgomery/Sasha Waddell's house in London; 14l ph Polly Wreford/Daniel Jasiak's apartment in Paris; 14r ph David Montgomery/Laura Bohn's apartment in New York designed by Laura Bohn Design Associates; 15 ph Alan Williams/Géraldine Prieur's apartment in Paris, an Interior Designer fascinated with color; 16l ph James Merrell/fabrics from Ian Mankin, trimmings from V. V. Rouleaux; 16r ph Alan Williams/The Arbuthnott family's house near Cirencester designed by Nicholas Arbuthnott, fabrics designed by Vanessa Arbuthnott; 17l James Merrell/an apartment in London (designed by François Gilles & Dominique Lubar, IPL Interiors; 17c A house in London designed by Charlotte Crosland Interiors; 17r ph James Merrell/Andrew Arnott and Karin Shack's house in Melbourne; 18 ph Alan Williams/Lisa Fine's apartment in Paris; 19a ph James Merrell/antique curtains from Antiques and Things; 19bl ph Polly Wreford/The Sawmills Studios; 19bc ph James Merrell/fabric from Pierre Frey; 19br ph Polly Wreford/The Sawmills Studios; 20 both ph David Montgomery/Sabina Fay Braxton's apartment in Paris; 21al ph David Montgomery/Annabel Astor's house in London is full of furniture and accessories designed exclusively for her OKA Direct Mail order catalogue; 21ar ph James Merrell/Christophe Gollut's apartment in London; 21ac&b Christian de Falbe's London home; 22al ph Christopher Drake/Marisa Cavalli's home in Milan; 22ac ph James Merrell/fabric and bobble fringe from Jane Churchill; 22ar Debby & Jeremy Amias' house in London designed by Carden Cunietti; 23 ph Christopher Drake/Marisa Cavalli's home in Milan; 24al ph Jan Baldwin/Laurence & Yves Sabourets' house in Brittany; 24ar ph James Merrell/Jane Jackson-stylist/designer; 24bl ph Chris Everard/Eric De Queker's apartment in Antwerp; 24br ph Simon Upton; 25 ph Ray Main/a house in London designed by Mark Guard Architects; 26–27 Christian de Falbe's London home; 28 Designed by Steven Roxburghe; 28–29 ph James Merrell/an apartment in New York, architect Campion A. Platt; 29 ph James Merrell/Kelly Hoppen's apartment in London; 30a ph Tom Leighton; 30bl ph James Merrell/an apartment in New York designed by James Biber of Pentagram with curtain design by Mary Bright; 30br ph Chris Everard/Eric De Queker's apartment in Antwerp; 31a ph Ray Main/Nello Renault's loft in Paris; 31b ph David Montgomery/Sasha Waddell's house in London; 32 Debby & Jeremy Amias' house in London designed by Carden Cunietti; 33 Designed by Steven Roxburghe; 34 ph James Merrell/Vincent Dané's house near Biarritz; 34–35 ph James Merrell/Sue and Andy A'Court's apartment in Blackheath, London; 35 ph James Merrell/A house designed by Mary Drysdale; 36 & 39 a house in London designed by François Gilles & Dominique Lubar, IPL Interiors; 40a ph Simon Upton; 40b ph David Montgomery/Blakes Lodging designed by Jeanie Blake www.picket.com/blakesBB/blakes.htm; 41al&ar ph Simon Upton; 41bl ph Henry Bourne; 41br ph James Merrell/Frédéric Méchiche's house near Toulon; 42l ph Simon Upton; 42r both Anne-Mette Fiil's house near Cambridge; 43 ph James Merrell/fabrics from Housemade; 46 ph Simon Upton; 48 Sheila Scholes' house near Cambridge; 49 ph James Merrell/Nigel Greenwood's apartment in London; 50al ph James Merrell/antique linen from Nicole Fabre, curtains by Reed Creative Services; 50bl ph James Merrell/fabric from Cath Kidston; 50r ph James Merrell/Christophe Gollut's apartment in London; 51a ph James Merrell/Interni Interior Design Consultancy; 51b ph James Merrell/Andrew Parr's house in Melbourne; 52, 53 & 55 Emily Todhunter's house in London designed by Todhunter Earle Interiors; 56 Curtain design by Sian and Annie Colley; 57al ph James Merrell/muslin from JAB, pole made to order; 57bl ph Andrew Wood/Mary Shaw's Sequana apartment in Paris; 57r ph James Merrell/an apartment in London designed by Ash Sakula Architects; 58al ph Christopher Drake/Enrica Stabile's house in Brunello; 58bl&r ph James Merrell/fabric from Shaker, pole from Artisan; 59 & 61 ph James Merrell/Hotel Villa Gallici Aix en Provence, France; 62 ph James Merrell/an apartment in London designed by Charles Rutherfoord; 63a ph Alan Williams/Interior Designer and Managing Director of the Société Yves Halard, Michelle Halard's own apartment in Paris; 63bl ph Simon Upton; 63bc ph James Merrell/designed by Larcombe and Solomon; 63br ph James Merrell/Vincent Dané's house near Biarritz; 64 ph Simon Upton; 65 ph Chris Everard/Lisa & Richard Frisch's apartment in New York designed by Patricia Seidman of Mullman Seidman Architects; 66 ph James Merrell; 67l ph Debi Treloar/The Zwirner's loft in New York; 67ar ph Andrew Wood/Brian Johnson's apartment in London designed by Johnson Naylor; 67cr ph David Montgomery/Sabina Fay Braxton's apartment in Paris; 67br ph Andrew Wood/Johanne Riss' house in Brussels; 68al ph Sandra Lane; 68ar ph Christopher Drake/Marisa Cavalli's home in Milan; 68bl ph Polly Wreford/Kimberley Watson's house in London; 68br Anne-Mette Fiil's house near Cambridge; 69 main & inset left Anne-Mette Fiil's house near Cambridge; 69 inset centre ph Polly Wreford; 69 inset right ph Sandra Lane; 70 ph Simon Upton; 70–71 Anne-Mette Fiil's house near Cambridge; 71 Sheila Scholes' house near Cambridge; 72 ph James Merrell; 74all Christian de Falbe's London home; 75 both Debby & Jeremy Amias' house in London designed by Carden Cunietti; 76 ph James Merrell/sheer fabric from Sanderson, ribbon from V. V. Rouleaux, expansion rod from John Lewis; 78al ph Ray Main; 78bl ph Alan Williams/Owner of Gloss, Pascale Bredillet's own apartment in London; 78ar ph James Merrell/fabric from Habitat, pole from McKinney & Co; 78br ph James Merrell/fabric, pole and fringe from John Lewis; 79 ph James Merrell/fabric from Pongees, ammonite knobs from John Lewis; 80 Debby & Jeremy Amias' house in London designed by Carden Cunietti; 81 ph James Merrell/architects, Ogawa Depardon, curtain designed by Mary Bright; 82al ph Sandra Lane; 82ac ph James Merrell/fabric from McKinney & Co, poles from Artisan, antique ring clips from Antiques & Things; 82ar ph James Merrell/ready-made curtains from The Source; 82b ph James Merrell/fabric from Sanderson, tension wire kit from Ikea; 83al Sheila Scholes' house near Cambridge; 83ac ph James Merrell/muslin from JAB, pole made to order; 83ar ph David Montgomery/designed by Todhunter Earle Interiors; 83bl ph Simon Upton; 83br ph James Merrell/both fabrics from KA International; 84 & 85 Sheila Scholes' house near Cambridge; 86al&bl ph James Merrell/Frédéric Méchiche's house near Toulon; 86acl ph Sandra Lane; 86acr ph James Merrell; 86ar ph Sandra Lane; 87a Christian de Falbe's London home; 87b Emily Todhunter's house in London designed by Todhunter Earle Interiors; 88 Curtain design by Sian and Annie Colley; 90 ph James Merrell/fabric from Sanderson, binding from John Lewis; 91al ph James Merrell/Khai & Sue Kellet; 91ac ph James Merrell/fabric from F. R. Street, felt from Muraspec, pole from Artisan; 91ar ph James Merrell/designed by François Gilles and Dominique Lubar, IPL Interiors; 91b ph James Merrell/fabric and bobble fringe from Jane Churchill; 92 Sheila Scholes' house near Cambridge; 94 ph David Montgomery/Blakes Lodging designed by Jeanie Blake www.picket.com/blakesBB/blakes.htm; 96–97 A house in London designed by Charlotte Crosland Interiors; 98, 98–99 & 99a A house in London designed by Charlotte Crosland Interiors; 99c & 99b Curtain design by Sian and Annie Colley; 100 Sheila Scholes' house near Cambridge; 101l ph Chris Everard/An apartment in Milan designed by Nicoletta Marazza; 101ar ph James Merrell/Vicente Wolfe's apartment, New York; 101cr Curtain design by Sian and Annie Colley; 101br ph Andrew Wood/Roger & Fay Oates' house in Eastnor; 102 ph Henry Bourne; 104 ph James Merrell/fabric from F. R. Street, felt from Muraspec, pole from Artisan; 104–105 & 105a Curtain design by Sian and Annie Colley; 105b A house in London designed by Charlotte Crosland Interiors; 106–107 & 109 Debby & Jeremy Amias' house in London designed by Carden Cunietti; 110–111 A house in London designed by Charlotte Crosland Interiors; 112l ph Ray Main/Malin Iovino's apartment in London; 112ar ph Christopher Drake/Enrica Stabile's house in Milano; 112br ph James Merrell/Vincent Dané's house near Biarritz; 113 Curtain design by Sian and Annie Colley; 114l ph Ray Main/Nello Renault's loft in Paris; 114ar ph James Merrell; 114br ph Henry Bourne; 115 & 117 ph Simon Upton; 118al ph Ray Main; 118ar ph David Montomery/The House of Crypton living laboratory apartment showroom in New York City designed by CR Studio Architects, PC; 118bl Emily Todhunter's house in London designed by Todhunter Earle Interiors; 118br & 119 A house in London designed by Charlotte Crosland Interiors; 120–121 A house in London designed by François Gilles and Dominique Lubar of IPL Interiors; 122 ph David Montgomery/Sasha Waddell's house in London; 123 ph Sandra Lane; 124 A house in London designed by François Gilles and Dominique Lubar of IPL Interiors; 125 Emily Todhunter's house in London designed by Todhunter Earle Interiors; 126 ph Debi Treloar/Victoria Andreae's house in London; 128a ph Christopher Drake/Enrica Stabile's house in Le Thor; 128bl Emily Todhunter's house in London designed by Todhunter Earle Interiors; 128br ph Christopher Drake/Diane Bauer's house near Cotignac; 129 ph Debi Treloar/Victoria Andreae's house in London; 130al ph Simon Upton; 130ar & 130bl Debby & Jeremy Amias' house in London designed by Carden Cunietti; 130br & 131 A house in London designed by François Gilles and Dominique Lubar of IPL Interiors; 132l Debby & Jeremy Amias' house in London designed by Carden Cunietti; 132r ph Catherine Gratwicke/Jeff McKay's apartment in New York; 133 ph Sandra Lane; 138 Debby & Jeremy Amias' house in London designed by Carden Cunietti; 140 Sheila Scholes' house near Cambridge; 143 Designed by Steven Roxburghe; 144 Sheila Scholes' house near Cambridge.

In addition to the designers and home owners mentioned above we would also like to thank the following: Nancy Braithwaite, Mr & Mrs Derald Ruttenberg; Beverly Jacomini, Wendy Harrop, Bruno & Hélène Lafforgue, Marie Kalt, Lena Proudlock, Liz Dougherty Pierce, K Russell Glover & Angela Miller and Tricia Foley.

# Index

Figures in *italics* indicate captions; those in **bold** indicate projects.

## ACKNOWLEDGMENTS

This book is the product of the considerable talents of the creative team put together
by RPS. I would like to thank everybody who has been involved along the way, in
particular Alison for asking me to be involved in the first place; Sophie for her
patience, editorial guidance, and eye for detail; Emily for the faultless picture
research; Ali for her elegant prose, and especially Lizzie for her exquisite watercolors.
Lucinda Ganderton